MW01196117

"Nicora Placa's *6 Tools for Colla*
useful content complemented w
to-use activities and protocols every coach will use. This book will be the go-to
for new coaches, experienced coaches, and anyone who supports them!"

John SanGiovanni
Howard County Public School System Mathematics Coordinator

"Everything I learned about quality math instruction I attribute to my work
with Nicora Placa. Through the lesson study framework, she was able to create
a safe and productive experience that allowed both teachers and administrators to learn from each other, and from our students. The student interview
process taught me the importance of understanding student thinking and
changed the way I questioned students. My hope is that *6 Tools for Collaborative Mathematics Coaching* will allow more coaches to provide their teachers
with engaging and impactful professional development, as I was so lucky to
experience."

Kathryn Bingman
Math Teacher

"In *6 Tools for Collaborative Mathematics Coaching*, Nicora Placa shares from
personal experiences and research how to make the most impact as a mathematics coach—utilizing the power of coaching teams. Throughout the book, you
will connect with stories from the field and explore a variety of tools and strategies that support teams collaborating and learning with one another. If you are
looking for new ways to deepen your mathematics coaching skills with collaborative teams, then you absolutely have the right book in your hands."

Mona Toncheff
NCSM Past President and Math Coach

"In *6 Tools for Collaborative Mathematics Coaching*, Nicora advocates for practical recommendations to generate sustainable growth in mathematics teaching
and learning. Nicora shares expert knowledge for developing professional
learning communities where mathematics coaching becomes a transformational
experience for everyone involved. *6 Tools* is an essential resource for mathematics coaches and instructional leaders at any point in their careers."

Brea Ratliff
Past President, Benjamin Banneker Association

"*6 Tools* tells the story of what it means to be an inspired mathematics coach guided by equity principles and the belief that all students can achieve to the highest levels. Both honest and wise, Nicora deftly outlines the work of coaches who center students' thinking and create a space for teachers to nurture their learning lives. This book will live on my desk with its well-worn and dog-eared pages, my go-to resource for all things coaching."

Polly Wagner
Math Coach and Consultant

"Nicora Placa's book, *6 Tools for Collaborative Mathematics Coaching*, is one of a kind. It is the perfect marriage of theory, research, and practical application. Instructional coaches will learn how to create a collaborative coaching culture in their school by using the authentic tools Nicora developed while working in K–12 schools. Nicora designed this book to be interactive and flexible, intentionally asking the reader to reflect on their own practice in schools, solidify their beliefs about learning and engage in action planning. This book is a must-read for all instructional coaches!"

Megan Gundogdu
Assistant Principal

"In this fresh and heartfelt resource for mathematics coaches, Nicora Placa introduces a new set of tools and strategies for making coaching more impactful. She introduces a framework for collaborative coaching and emphasizes the importance of students and teachers constructing their own understanding as they engage as learners. She also provides many examples of what the process looks like and frames a clear vision for how to take coaching to a more collaborative place."

Diane Sweeney
author of *The Essential Guide for Student-Centered Coaching*

"Nicora Placa's *6 Tools for Collaborative Mathematics Coaching* is a book geared for coaches, but it is more than that. I recommend this book to both teachers and administrators as well. It is THE resource on how to learn to work together in a supportive and goal-oriented team."

Byron Licari
Math Teacher

"*6 Tools for Collaborative Mathematics Coaching* is a great resource to increase collaboration in the classroom and with teacher teams. Not only does it have great strategies, but the directions and facilitating questions makes this book a tool that will help when facilitating coaching conversations around collaboration."

Natevidad Casas
Secondary Math Coordinator

6

TOOLS for Collaborative
Mathematics Coaching

TOOLS
for Collaborative Mathematics Coaching

Nicora Placa

Foreword by Elham Kazemi

Stenhouse Publishers
Portsmouth, New Hampshire

www.stenhouse.com

Stenhouse Publishers
www.stenhouse.com

Copyright © 2023 by Nicora Placa

All rights reserved. Except for pages in the appendix, which can be photocopied for classroom use, no part of this publication may be reproduced or transmitted in any form or by any means, electronic or mechanical, including photocopy, or any information storage and retrieval system, without permission from the publisher.

Every effort has been made to contact copyright holders and students for permission to reproduce borrowed material. We regret any oversights that may have occurred and will be pleased to rectify them in subsequent reprints of the work.

Figures 4.2a and 4.2b, IM Implementation Reflection Tool by Shelby Danks, Jennifer Wilson, Max Ray-Riek, and Liz Ramirez. © 2021 Illustrative Mathematics. Used by permission of Illustrative Mathematics.

Cataloging-in-Publication data on file with the Library of Congress

ISBN: 978-1-62531-384-3(paperback); 978-1-62531-385-0(ebook)

Cover design by Cindy Butler
Interior design by Jill Shaffer
Typesetting by Eclipse Publishing Services

Printed in the United States of America

This book is printed on paper certified by third-party standards for sustainably managed forestry.

29 28 27 26 25 24 23   4371   9 8 7 6 5 4 3 2 1

To my mom,
the greatest teacher of all.
Everything I am is because of you.

CONTENTS

FOREWORD

Elham Kazemi, PhD

Professor, Mathematics Education, University of Washington

D o you have a vision for how you would like to work with your colleagues as a coach in a school but are not exactly sure what kinds of norms have to be in place, how you have to see each other as teammates, and how to get there? Are you frustrated with the limits of individual coaching and wondering how teachers can "learn together, engage in risk-taking, and build relationships?" Are you interested in thinking deeply about how to foster authentic collaboration? If you find yourself thinking about these questions, then you've found the right book. Nicora Placa begins by inviting you to think about an idea she calls "collaborative coaching," or working alongside teams of teachers to foster both their learning and your own. In *6 Tools for Collaborative Mathematics Coaching*, Nicora takes seriously the deeply relational work that teaching is, and by extension, that coaching has to be.

This book is well written, accessible, and grounded in principles for teacher learning. I don't think we pay enough attention to how teachers learn. They are not just receptacles that need to be told what to do. Teachers are sensemakers who need intentional opportunities to learn from and with others. So I found myself nodding along as Nicora shared principles of learning that guide us when engaging in coaching. I'll repeat them here because thinking about how we create school cultures to enable this kind of learning for teachers is vital to making schools better places for students and for teachers. Nicora suggests teachers learn when they

- have opportunities to construct new knowledge on their own.
- have opportunities and time to explore different ideas and practice new skills.

- are encouraged to take risks and make mistakes.
- have opportunities to examine and discuss other teachers' work and strategies.
- sometimes work in whole groups, small groups, and individually with the coach.

In this book, Nicora will help you imagine, develop, and refine how you put these principles into practice. What can you do to invite teachers into creating learning communities for each other? The specifics are nicely organized around a set of tools that coaches can use in a variety of contexts, but all share a laser-like focus on the importance of nurturing teacher learning by attending to students' thinking and experiences in the classroom. That's the crucial approach that I found so compelling throughout the book.

There's so much to love about how *6 Tools* is constructed. Take for example the first tool, which is about how you build teams. Nicora provides a vision for what authentic collaboration means and then provides concrete ideas for how you orchestrate discussions with teachers about their own collaboration; how you make explicit the initial expectations and norms you should have for working together. You'll find yourself swept into the vignettes she uses because they enable you to step into coaching contexts with her and understand what she notices, how she thinks, and why she makes the moves she does. But nothing is ever easy or straightforward in the messy real world of schools, so Nicora is clear about the challenges that arise. She helps you anticipate those challenges and think about how to respond so they don't derail the important work you are doing.

Real and meaningful collaboration that actually makes a difference for teachers and students is something that coaches continually work on. With each of the learning tools that Nicora describes–student interviews, classroom visits, learning walks, rehearsals, and lesson study–she helps you think about how to frame the learning and draw on these tools, not in isolation, but coordinated with one another. After reading this book, you'll have a toolbox of different ways to support teacher learning, and you'll be able to think about which tool to use when. Because each tool focuses the team on student learning, which is the key to supporting teacher learning, you and your colleagues can really transform classrooms together.

Throughout the book, I love that Nicora helps you imagine how to make your commitments to teacher learning come to life. For example, when she talks about visiting classrooms or doing learning walks, she doesn't just say "spend a lot of time in classrooms building relationships." Nicora goes further to help you think about the purpose of low-inference note taking, ways you might try out a follow-up conversation, the importance of thinking through the tasks that you might see and anticipating what students might do, and how to develop a guiding question. She makes insightful suggestions and then helps you visualize her guiding ideas by always providing a specific example that puts you into the work directly, such as the actual notes from a classroom learning walk. You'll find yourself eagerly planning how you'll use the tools in your context, with your colleagues, while you read.

If you are ready to deepen your coaching practice, grab this book with your colleagues and jump in so you can figure out what's next in your school and build meaningful learning experiences for and with teachers.

ACKNOWLEDGMENTS

This book is about collaboration, and although writing is a solo endeavor in many ways, none of this work would have been possible without so many different people who I have been fortunate enough to cross paths with in this lifetime.

First and foremost, this book was inspired by the many teams of teachers and administrators that I have worked with over the years in different schools. You made me a better coach, a better teacher, and a better mathematician. Thank you for opening your schools and your classrooms to me. It has meant the world that you trusted me.

To my One World family. Trish Wynne, you were the first principal to believe in me and hire me as a coach when I started out on my own. I could not be any prouder that you allowed me to be a small part of your school's journey. Kam Waugh-Gordon and Nicole Conlisk, working with you to help coach the One World math team was a joy. To all the math teachers at One World that I worked with when I was first learning about these ideas, thank you for your kindness and grace.

To my VNA family, the team I have worked with the longest. Carol Ann Gilligan, Ann Reynolds, and Melanie Marino have been a dream team of administrators. Megan Gundogdu, it seems fitting that we met years ago at a PD. I loved teaching alongside you, and it has been a privilege to watch you become an administrator that I would have loved to work for as a teacher. You allowed me to test out ideas and helped make our vision a reality. It is an added bonus that you are a wonderful friend. Christie Galasso, I have enjoyed working with you over the years and watching you make the transition to coaching. Elga Barber, Kathryn Bingman, Jen Covino, Elisa Hernandez, Chis Lupinacci, Bryon Licari, and Lauren Molisani—as the 5–8 math team, you have been trailblazers in changing the way kids learn math. I wish everyone could visit your classrooms and see the amazing learning that occurs within those walls. I have learned so much from you all. To all the teachers at VNA, thank you for allowing me to be a part of your classrooms and your lives.

To all the students I have worked with—elementary and middle school students, undergraduate and graduate students—you have changed me in a way I could never have imagined. I hope I honored your thinking and made you see math differently. You have made me see the world differently, and I will never be the same.

To my online math community. When I started blogging, I never expected to be received with such love. Dan Meyer retweeted one of my blogs and changed the course of it. Christopher Danielson sat with me on a conference hall floor and encouraged me to find my own path when I was unsure of what to do. Robert Kaplinsky came to one of my talks and gave me feedback on public speaking when I was just starting out. There are so many more of you that I have enjoyed sharing ideas with online and in person. I can't thank you enough for the ways you pushed my thinking and allowed the Internet to be a positive space for me.

To my Hunter family. I strongly believed academia wasn't for me, but you proved me wrong, over and over again. Thanks to all of you. From the executive committee—Jody Polleck, Melissa Shieble, and Jason Wirtz—who never made me feel like a junior faculty member and continue to support and advise me. To Brian Collins, who helps me keep things in perspective. To Laura Baecher, who fostered my growth and hosted writing retreats in which I completed chapters of this book. To Jenny Tuten, who hired me and started me on this journey. To Terrie Epstein, who was the best department chair. And to Karen Koellner, who believed in me from the start and has given me countless opportunities to learn and grow, from coteaching with me to placing me on grants. I loved our Thursday visits to schools, and you have always inspired me to think outside the box in how we support teachers. Nanette Seago, you aren't part of my Hunter family, but you are a big part of my growth as a researcher, and your honoring of teachers in our work has been an inspiration. You and Karen will always be my favorite conference buddies.

To my NYU family. Marty Simon, you changed the way I think about learning. Being your graduate student was one of the most challenging and rewarding experiences of my career. Orit Zaslavsky, you taught me about professional learning and made NYU feel like a home by hosting the most amazing dinners and brunches. Jasmine Ma, I still think of your advice about writing when I sit down at my laptop. Arnon Avitzur, I wouldn't have survived the program without you. I am so grateful for all our conversations about learning and teaching. Barb Dougherty, I met you when I was a graduate student at NYU, and you gave me a vision of how to translate research to practice. You continue to inspire me, and getting to work alongside you recently in providing PD and coaching has been an incredible experience.

To the mathematics education researchers and practitioners whose work I have read and learned from: I have been inspired by so many of you, and the ideas presented here build on your hard work. A special thank you to Elham Kazemi. Your research on student thinking and teacher learning continues to push my thinking and has influenced so much of the work I try to do in schools. I remember talking with you at a Stenhouse event back when this book was still an idea, and your kindness and encouragement meant so much to me. I am deeply honored by your foreword.

To my Stenhouse family. I can still remember my first meeting with Tracy Zager, who saw me as a writer long before I did. You promised me that I could write the book I wanted—this is the book I wanted and more. You made my ideas come to life and made me see the beauty in the writing process. You made my ideas shine and my love of coaching sing. I can never thank you enough for your patience and your support. You made me believe in this book, even through a pandemic, and helped me see that my words meant something. Thank you for also forgiving my constant need to put two spaces at the end of a sentence. To the production team—Shannon St. Peter, Steph Levy, Cindy Butler, Mark Corsey, and Eclipse Publishing—and everyone in editorial, marketing, and operations, thank you for making this book possible.

To my friends. I am so lucky to be surrounded by the most amazing friends, who continue to amaze me with their accomplishments, guidance, and love. I know you are sick of hearing me talk about when this book is coming out, so here it is. Thank you all for your support along the way. To Caroline DeGraff, my fiercest defender and lifelong friend, thanks for continuing to believe I could do this. To Liz Monaghan, thank you for your unconditional support, and thank you for allowing me to test out ideas with your children. We have come a long way from me writing papers furiously in our campus apartment the night before they were due. And to Thê-Vàn Maxence Tran, thank you for taking my author photo and for making the best baked goods around.

To my family. I have been blessed with the most wonderful and supportive family. To my brother, the mathematical genius, who will work out math problems on napkins with me at family dinner. To my father, who may not remember what college I work at but is proud to tell anyone about the accomplishments of his kids. To my sister-in-law, who takes care of us all and makes every family gathering special. To my sister, who is my best friend and favorite travel buddy. And to the new generation of women they have brought into our family. To my nieces, I will always be one of your biggest cheerleaders and your greatest advocates. Don't ever let anyone take away your independence and sparkle. I know you will do wonderful things in this world, and I cannot wait to watch you take it on.

Finally, thanks to my momma, a veteran NYC elementary school teacher who shared her love of teaching and learning with me. I am proud to follow in your footsteps. You raised the three of us to believe we could do anything. You will always be the voice in my head cheering me on and making me believe I am invincible. I could not imagine my life without you as my mother. Thank you for everything.

HOW TO USE THIS BOOK

When I started coaching, I searched for a how-to guide to start my work but couldn't find one. This book grew out of my desire to provide that resource for others and is what I wished I'd had when I began my work. I hope that the tools provide some guidance for you on your coaching journey.

You can read this book successfully in many ways:

- From start to finish
- About the tools that are the most interesting to you
- On your own
- With other coaches

If you are not going to read from start to finish, I recommend you read the introduction to get an overview of collaborative coaching and then read about *Tool 1: Building Teams*, which will help you foster learning communities. Exploring these sections first will help set the groundwork for successful implementation of the other tools. From there, feel free to skip to the tools that intrigue you most.

That said, I organized the book by placing the tools in the order I often implement them when I am working with a new team of teachers. For example, I find that *Tool 2: Student Interviews* provides a nice entry point for a team before I begin using *Tool 4: Learning Walks* with them. However, your experience and knowledge of your teams and their history together may prompt you to change this order.

I also created the 6 Tools website (https://nicoraplaca.com/6tools/), which has a variety of resources to support you as you implement the different tools. It includes links to websites, videos, and other curated materials that deepen and expand upon the ideas presented in the book. I encourage you to explore this website and adapt and modify the resources as you see fit.

As you move along with your coaching, it can be important to find a community of coaches to collaborate with. Coaching can be isolating work if you do not have others to share and learn from, whether bouncing ideas off one another or strategizing how best to adapt or modify tools for your context. You may already have this community in your district. If so, that is great. If not, you may want to join the National Council of Supervisors of Mathematics (NCSM), a national professional organization focused on mathematics education leadership, to find others in your position.

As you grow with your community, my suggestion is to work through the questions at the end of each section together and share your ideas with one another. I would also suggest that you schedule check-ins where you share both successes to celebrate and challenges you are facing and then brainstorm solutions together.

I also hope that we can create an online community of coaches so that we can share our work with one another. One way we can do this is through social media, using the hashtag #6ToolsForMathCoaches. You can also reach out to me directly at @NicoraPlaca.

I look forward to learning from all of you as you adapt and modify these tools for your contexts.

WHAT IS COLLABORATIVE COACHING?

Several years ago, the assistant principal of a K–8 school called me about some of the challenges she was having at her school. "I have a great team of teachers. They work hard, they have wonderful relationships with their students, and they are experienced, but our math scores are low. We purchased a new math program that we feel reflects our beliefs about inquiry-based instruction, but our teachers are struggling with implementing it. My background is in ELA, and although I want to support the teachers, I'm not an expert on the content. I need help. Do you think you can work with us?"

After meeting with the assistant principal (AP) and her team, I decided to take on the work even though I knew it would be challenging, because I believed in the mission and vision of the school. The administration was really pushing for student-centered, inquiry-based math instruction; they believed in collaboration; they weren't looking for a quick fix; and they were willing to put in the time and effort to support their teachers. Plus, I liked the people I met. Taken together, these conditions seemed to set us up to be successful.

At first, I worked on building relationships with the teachers. I got to know them. I asked lots of questions. I listened. While building these relationships, I worked with teachers individually on planning lessons. A meeting with an individual teacher might consist of us unpacking and modifying the new curriculum. We might coteach a lesson and debrief after. Sometimes, the two of us would examine student work and plan next steps. Other times, I observed lessons, and we developed feedback together afterward. The conversations were rich, and the teachers and I learned interesting things about teaching and learning. It seemed like things were going smoothly.

However, the assistant principal had a meeting with me halfway into the year. "Nicora, I don't get it. When you are here, we have these deep conversations, we see teachers lead great student-based lessons, and we all seem to be on the same page, but when I'm doing observations, I'm still seeing the same chalk-and-talk that we are trying to move away from. What's going on?"

I had no idea. I was confused and frustrated. Even more, I felt ineffective. I didn't have "resistant teachers." I didn't have an unsupportive admin team. I had resources and time and all the things I asked for. I had great conditions to be an effective coach, yet I was failing.

The assistant principal and I brainstormed what might be going on. We asked the teachers what they thought the disconnect was, and we talked to the admin team. We started to realize that although some shifts had occurred in beliefs and attitudes about teaching math, these beliefs were conditional. For example, teachers were starting to believe that students had interesting ideas about math even before they were exposed to the mathematics in school. They were starting to believe that a lesson did not necessarily need to include direct modeling of a new skill. However, when we dug deeper, we found they believed these ideas were true only *sometimes*. Students didn't need direct modeling, for example, but this was true only at the beginning or end of the unit. Students brought their own ideas to the topics, but only for the lessons that we worked on together.

We also concluded that me working with individual teachers might not be the most efficient use of our time. The learning that was occurring with one teacher had to be re-created for the others. If a teacher left the school, our learning left with that teacher. In addition, we were missing out on the exchange of ideas that occurs when we discuss things as a larger group and learn from each other's strategies and work. It was as if a classroom teacher worked one-on-one with each student in their class instead of facilitating learning with the whole class or small groups.

We decided that we needed to work collectively and collaboratively if we were going to see impactful change. We researched different tools and structures that could help us do some of this collaboration. We read the literature, and we asked colleagues what they were doing that was making an impact. After we investigated some different options, we decided to begin with a modified form of *lesson study*: a process that originated in Japan where teachers work in teams to plan, teach, observe, analyze, and revise lessons.

After several lesson studies over the course of a school year, we noticed small shifts that later led to bigger shifts. The main change that affected everything else was that teachers grew more willing to take risks. They were willing to try something new during a lesson and look at their experience as a learning opportunity, even if it didn't go as planned. They began to spontaneously invite their colleagues for feedback on lessons when they were trying something new or when they anticipated that students might struggle, not only when they had a lesson they thought was "perfect." They reached out to their colleagues because they wanted help thinking through challenges with a thought partner. They brought student work to meetings and said, "No one got it. What happened? What do I do now?" They leaned on each other for support when they struggled with teaching a challenging concept. When they read about a new strategy or were confronted with a problem they couldn't solve, they said, "Can we do a lesson study on this?"

As we continued with lesson study the following school year, the culture changed from one where teachers shared only "best practices" during professional development (PD) or did intervisitations on "model lessons" to one where teachers wanted to hear about lessons that didn't go well or struggles someone else was having because it was in these situations where they felt they learned the most.

In retrospect, we realized that the changes occurred because we leveraged the team and not just individuals. Through lesson study, we were able to work collaboratively to explore different ideas we were curious about. The AP, teachers, and I worked through planning and implementing lessons together. We all brought different strengths to the meetings and learned from each other. The AP allowed herself to be vulnerable; I often discussed the mistakes I made in lessons and how we learned from them; and teachers became comfortable sharing the parts of their teaching they felt less sure about. Lesson study is just one of several collaborative coaching tools that can create opportunities for teams to learn together, engage in risk-taking, and build relationships. Using these tools to create an environment where we valued mistakes changed our work together, and this cultural shift, in turn, started to change the work with students.

HOW DO TEACHERS LEARN BEST?

When I began thinking about ways to create more of these collaborative learning opportunities for teachers, it helped to realize I didn't need to start at square one. I already knew a lot about creating collaborative learning communities for students. I started wondering about how I might adapt what I knew about teaching math to elementary and middle school students to my new context—coaching math teachers. What helps foster learning with students? What would it mean to use some of these strategies to design learning opportunities for teachers?

Try going through the same process I did. Take a minute and jot down your answers to the following questions.

STOP and JOT

 What are the principles that guide your teaching of math?

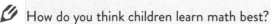 How do you think children learn math best?

I've created a list here. Is your list similar? What might you add from your experiences in the classroom?

STUDENT LEARNING OCCURS WHEN

- Students have opportunities to construct knowledge on their own as opposed to following a model of how to do the problem.
- Students have opportunities and time to explore different ideas and practice new skills.
- Students are encouraged to take risks and make mistakes.
- Students have opportunities to examine and discuss other students' work and strategies.
- Students sometimes work in whole groups, small groups, and individually with the teacher.

Now let's think about teacher learning. How would applying what we know about students impact our coaching and work with teachers? What if we changed "students" to "teachers" in the previous statements?

TEACHER LEARNING OCCURS WHEN

- Teachers have opportunities to construct knowledge on their own as opposed to following a model of how to teach.
- Teachers have opportunities and time to explore different ideas and practice new skills.
- Teachers are encouraged to take risks and make mistakes.
- Teachers have opportunities to examine and discuss other teachers' work and strategies.
- Teachers sometimes work in whole groups, small groups, and individually with the coach.

When you look at these two lists, what do you notice? I notice that many of the principles we use to guide learning for students can be transferred to how we guide learning for teachers. If we believe students need chances to construct their own understanding of mathematical concepts instead of being told what to do, it seems to follow that teachers also need opportunities to construct their own understanding of teaching strategies instead of being told what to do. Of course, the learning is not entirely parallel. For example, teachers bring a completely different set of prior experiences to their learning than students, and this knowledge needs to be valued and incorporated into learning activities. However, many of the overall conditions needed for learning remain the same.

Let's go back to the idea of lesson study. How does it align to the principles listed earlier? One important feature of lesson study is that the structure allowed us to build lessons together instead of someone "modeling" a lesson. Lesson study gave teachers opportunities to explore different ideas and practice these new skills. When we were planning, we chose difficult topics where we knew there would be some missteps, and we learned from them. In fact, we encouraged the team to take risks. We chose topics for these lessons that we knew were challenging for students. Lesson study also allowed for opportunities to discuss different ideas the team members brought to both the planning and analysis of the lesson. During lesson study, teachers worked in small grade-band groups with me, as the coach. However, they also had opportunities to work individually with me and to share with the whole group what they learned in their small groups. Lesson study met all the principles mentioned previously.

I find this list of principles helpful when I am choosing a tool to use with teachers. I look through the list and ask myself whether the tool is aligned with these ideas or whether I could adapt it further. Sometimes I need to modify my plan so we have more opportunities for practice. Other times, I need to create more risk-taking opportunities.

Learning to coach in this way forced me to step back and be the facilitator and not just the sharer of best practices or research. I felt like I was going through the same process I'd gone through as a new teacher, when I'd first learned how to create conditions for students to construct their own mathematical understanding rather than tell them how to get the answers by explaining or demonstrating. I began to think of my coaching role as consisting of the following:

- Building relationships not just between the teachers and myself but also among teams of teachers and between teachers and administrators
- Creating a culture where risk-taking is rewarded and encouraged and where we believe that we learn from challenges
- Carefully designing activities (lesson study, learning walks, etc.) that provide entry points for all participants to create their own knowledge
- Creating time and opportunities to practice and explore new strategies
- Listening, facilitating, and guiding the discussion that took place during these activities with a specific goal in mind
- Checking for understanding throughout the process
- Strategically choosing when to work with teachers in a whole group, small group, and individually because different tiers of support serve different purposes

I should point out that I just described my ideal world. In reality, we know that as coaches, we have other demands placed on us and it is not possible to define your role without addressing these other outside pressures. But I thought it was important for me to envision the role and then push myself to make it happen as best as I could. I encourage you to do the same. Think about what coaching means to you. What do *you* think needs to be done to improve student learning through effective coaching? Then try to stay as true to your ideals as you can, even as other demands are put on you. It will help to be strong in your vision as you make choices and decisions and choose your battles.

This ideal list also does not address the various types of coaching roles we may have. For example, building relationships among teams can look different when we are school-based coaches than when we are district-based coaches. As you read through the next section, think about your own coaching responsibilities and contexts and how they may impact the ways in which you implement the principles.

DIFFERENT TYPES OF COACHING ROLES

Coaching takes many shapes. Next are some coaching models I have seen. You may want to add to the list based on your experiences.

- We may be a full-time coach or a part-time coach with teaching responsibilities.
- We may be a brand-new coach or an experienced coach.
- We may have experience coaching other content areas but are new to coaching math.
- We may be responsible for working with many schools or may be a coach in one school.
- We may coach only math, or we may coach multiple content areas.
- We may work with mostly new teachers, or we may work with veteran teachers.
- We may have existing relationships with the teachers we are working with or be brand new to them.
- We may have been successful math teachers but haven't received support about teaching adults.
- We may be in a school or district that has a history or culture around coaching, or we may be the first coach in that school or district.
- We may be working with teachers who are open to coaching or skeptical of it.
- We may have opportunities to collaborate with other coaches, or we may not.
- We may share the same vision as the administration, or we may not.

- We may be expected to be a curriculum specialist for a particular program, or we may be expected to help create a new curriculum.
- We may be given other responsibilities in addition to our coaching roles, such as intervention, technology, or administrative work.

Think about where you are on this list. In the lesson study example from earlier, I was a more experienced math coach working with experienced teachers in an environment where most teachers were open to coaching and where I shared the vision of the administration. I visited the school once a week and had no intervention or administrative opportunities. I've also been in situations that are the opposite of that one.

I started my coaching journey accidently. I taught at a small school with a lot of new teachers. The principal knew the new teachers needed mentoring, so she designed my schedule in a way that allowed me to teach my math classes in the morning and then coach the new teachers in the afternoon. Later, I took a position as a full-time math coach in a brand-new school where I also had intervention and administrative responsibilities, and I did not share the vision of the administration. I've been brought in as an outside consultant/coach for multiple schools. I see some schools once a week and work with others once a month. I've facilitated professional development for math coaches and administrators at the district level and coached coaches at the school level. These schools and districts had different cultures surrounding coaching—different needs and different strengths. I still do both school-level and district-level coaching. In addition, I also coach preservice teachers who are in clinically rich graduate programs.

All of these situations are unique and present their own affordances and challenges. These different contexts and environments keep the work interesting for me. They also remind me that there is no one-size-fits-all solution that I could use in each of these scenarios and recommend to you. The reality of the work is that it is complicated and unique and interesting—just like teaching. Each classroom is unique, and each context brings its own dilemmas. We can give teachers tools, but they need to take their teacher knowledge and magic and make the tools work for their contexts. My goal with this book is the same. I'll share some tools and how I have used them, and then you can take your coaching knowledge and magic and choose and modify the tools so that they will work in your environment and build on the work you already do. I'll provide suggestions and ideas to think about, and my hope is that, after you try out ideas and modify them, you'll share what you've learned. Just like teachers need opportunities to collaborate and discuss their work, so do we. I encourage you to find other coaches with whom to talk through these ideas.

In each section, we will explore a different tool. You can read them in order or skip around to the ones that sound appealing to you. At the end of every section, you'll find questions to think about. I invite you to take some time to pause and reflect. You might want to keep a journal and handwrite your thoughts, or maybe you would rather create a file on your laptop. For me, writing helps me clarify my thoughts, and I often learn through the process of writing. Others might find it more helpful to talk these questions through with another coach or colleague. Do what works for you.

Let's get started!

REFLECTING on LEARNING

- If it were up to you, what would an ideal coaching day look like? How would you know you were successful? What are the challenges in making that vision happen?

- Make a list of all the different roles and responsibilities you have as a coach. How does it align with your ideal day? Are there any adjustments you can make to align it more closely?

- How often do you work with teacher teams versus work individual teachers? What might be the benefit of each type of work?

- Why do you think lesson study was so powerful in the school described?

EXPLORING the LITERATURE

One of the things I love most about coaching is the chance to read more about teaching and learning. Exploring research studies or books and articles written by other educators allows us to stand on the shoulders of others who have done the work instead of starting from scratch. Reading also allows us to make convincing arguments when we need to justify or support the work we are doing. I have found that referring to the literature can be particularly helpful when working with administrators or district-level personnel. In each section, I will provide some suggested research articles and professional books that you can use to learn more about the different tools.

When I went to the literature on coaching, the NCTM Research Brief (McGatha et al. 2015) titled "The Impact of Mathematics Coaching on Teachers and Students" was a helpful resource. This research summary suggests that one-on-one coaching that is *less directive* in nature is more powerful in affecting teacher change than one-on-one coaching that is *more directive*. *More directive* coaching includes modeling lessons and sharing resources, whereas *less directive* coaching includes engaging teachers in reflective activities. Just as when we work with students, the more we let teachers create their own knowledge through carefully guided experiences, the more impactful the learning is.

In terms of group coaching practices, the literature suggests that it is important for group meetings to be held regularly and have a specific focus related to practice, such as analyzing student work or exploring specific teaching strategies. Gibbons and Cobb (2017) identified four potentially productive activities to consider when working with teacher teams: engaging in mathematics, examining student work, analyzing classroom video, and engaging in lesson study.

I am often asked about whether the research says whether group coaching is more effective than one-one-one coaching. I don't think that's quite the right question to be asking. We don't need to claim that one is better than the other—just recognize that they serve different purposes. I find it more helpful to share the research that supports collaborative models. For example, research suggests that instructional coaching that is collaborative and supports the learning of the whole team plays a strong role in schoolwide reform (Desimone and Pak 2017; Gibbons et al. 2017; Mangin and Dunsmore 2015). Teachers need opportunities to learn together and develop shared meanings about teaching (Borko 2004; Grossman et al. 2001; King and Newmann 2001).

If you want to read a compelling case of an elementary mathematics coach whose work supported teams of teachers, look at the article "Developing Collective Capacity to Improve Mathematics Instruction: Coaching as a Lever for School-Wide Improvement" by Gibbons, Kazemi, and Lewis (2017). The researchers describe the work of a coach who used Math Labs, which are similar to the lesson study–inspired work you will read about in Tool 6, to provide opportunities for collective learning. The study provides a strong argument for how collective coaching can transform teaching and learning in a school.

Finally, many professional books on coaching are not based on research studies but do incorporate research-based practices. I have found these resources helpful in my coaching work, and they complement the strategies discussed in this book. Elena Aguilar's *The Art of Coaching Teams: Building Resilient Communities That Transform Schools* (2016) is not specifically about math teams but does focus on coaching teams of teachers, which may be helpful if your role extends to teachers in other subjects. Diane Sweeney has also written extensively about coaching and has several books that focus on centering students and student learning in your coaching. You may want to start with *The Essential Guide for Student-Centered Coaching* (2020) (written with Leanna S. Harris). This book is also not specific to math teachers but contains some valuable advice and strategies for your work. If you are looking for books specific to math, Lucy West and Antonia Cameron's book *Agents of Change: How Content Coaching Transforms Teaching and Learning* (2013) is focused on mathematics coaching. West and Cameron focus more on individual coaching of teachers, which may be helpful as you support the collaborative work described here with individual coaching. Finally, *Mathematics Coaching and Collaboration in a PLC at Work* (2018) by Kanold et al. provides systems and structures for leading professional learning communities.

BUILDING TEAMS
Fostering a Learning Community

Early in my teaching career, I taught math in a small middle school that had the most amazing culture. I learned more from one year of being in that learning community than I did in all of graduate school. Most of us were newer teachers, and we relied on each other to improve our practice. We visited one another's classrooms, shared resources, cocreated lessons, discussed student work, and provided critical feedback about each other's teaching. We also were given opportunities to take on leadership roles. For example, we coached each other through hybrid coaching roles, we interviewed new hires as a team, we designed and facilitated professional developments, and we mentored our new teachers. Our students were successful, morale among teachers was high, and we looked forward to coming to work every day. Then, something happened that shifted the whole culture of the school.

The principal was offered the opportunity to have two outside consultants come to the school once a week. One was to support us in math, and the other, in reading and writing. On paper, this sounded like a great plan. An outside perspective on what was going on in the school would be helpful, and we were looking forward to learning from these experienced coaches.

In reality, though, the first visit from these two consultants was a nightmare. They visited our classrooms, barely looked at us, took notes, and then gathered us in a room to report what they saw (mostly what they thought was wrong) and what the plan was for their work moving forward. It was a terrible introduction for a number of reasons, but the biggest mistake was that they dismissed the informal learning communities we had created. They tried to start from scratch to create formal coaching relationships and professional learning communities instead of building on what was already there . . . and working.

The mood shifted almost immediately. We were tense and nervous when the coaches visited our rooms. We stopped taking risks and instead made sure we had the "perfect" lesson prepared when they were scheduled to visit. Our conversations in professional development and team meetings were not authentic and instead consisted of us trying to say what we thought they wanted to hear. The learning culture that we had created was gone.

Even the students resented the presence of these "experts." One time, a coach interrupted my lesson, came up to the board, took the marker out of my hand, and started explaining to the students what I was doing wrong. I was humiliated. I remember slinking into a seat in the back of the room, feeling like many students do when this happens to them in math class. Later in the day, I found out a group of my eighth-grade boys locked her in the math closet. When I talked to the students, they kept saying, "We know we shouldn't have, but she was just so rude to you." It turned into an interesting opportunity for us to discuss how we feel when someone with power uses that power to make us feel so little.

In defense of the consultants who came to my building, I think they had good intentions. They genuinely wanted to improve student learning, and the ideas they were trying to share were important and valuable. In addition, they felt a sense of urgency and wanted to get to work right away. But their delivery was problematic. By not taking the time to build relationships at the start, they weren't able to convey these ideas, and we, as teachers, weren't able to receive them.

Soon after these consultants came to the school, teachers started to leave, and I found myself moving on as well.

WHAT ARE THE CHARACTERISTICS OF AN EFFECTIVE LEARNING COMMUNITY?

I've talked to many teachers who have had similar experiences. When I start as a consultant in schools, sometimes teachers are initially resistant because they have had an experience like this—a time where their work and knowledge weren't valued. They had a coach or administrator who came into the school and tried to change things immediately and without their input. Someone didn't take time to get to know them or look at the great things that were already going on and try to build from there.

This dynamic is not all that different from what goes on in a math classroom. If you don't take the time to create a positive learning environment and build relationships with your students, it is difficult to engage them in learning math. That's why, as teachers, we spend so much time building community in our classrooms at the start of the year. I have found this investment is just as important in coaching. Although the individual relationships I build with teachers are important, I also need to build a learning community within the team.

When thinking about how to build these communities as a coach, I started with what I knew. I thought back to that teacher learning community I described earlier, before the consultant visit, and tried to identify what made it effective. Then I was able to think about what strategies I could use to create those conditions. It might be helpful for you to go through a similar process. Take a couple of minutes and think about the best learning community you have been a part of. For some of you, this may be a community at a school you worked at; for others, it may have been a community from your undergraduate or graduate work; for yet others, it may be an online community you belong to. Try to identify a community where your thinking changed as a result of being part of the group. After you have a clear picture of this community in mind, answer the following questions.

STOP and JOT

What did the community look like? Did you meet in person? How often? For how long? Were the meetings formally scheduled or informally scheduled? Who were the members of the community? How did one join the community? How were new members brought in?

(continued)

What did your meetings sound like? What did you talk about? Did you use protocols, or did the conversation emerge naturally? Did you use agendas? Set goals?

How did you feel during these conversations? After these conversations? How did you feel if someone challenged an idea you had? What was the mood or tone of the discussions?

After you've had time to describe the details of the community, look back over your notes and try to answer the following question:

What were the characteristics that made the community successful?

Following is a list of qualities of effective learning communities that I have gathered from being a part of different communities, visiting different schools, and talking with teachers about their experiences. As you read through, think about whether these features were also true for your learning community.

CHARACTERISTICS OF AN EFFECTIVE LEARNING COMMUNITY

- Clear goal/purpose
- Shared vision
- Trust among members
- Willingness to take risks
- Shared norms

- Joy
- Passion
- Collaboration

These characteristics help me set goals and begin work with new groups or teams. I start by using this list to choose initial activities that will build an effective learning community. I also use this list to think about what systems and structures I may need to leverage, help create, or support so that we can achieve our goals. For example, if my goal is to build a community that values risk-taking, I may ask everyone to bring a lesson that didn't go well to a team meeting so that we can talk about our mistakes instead of only sharing our best lessons. I can use an existing structure (the team meeting) to create an activity (sharing our mistakes) that supports our goal (building a community that values risk-taking).

This process of visualizing and articulating what an ideal learning community looks like is something you may want to do with a new group of teachers that you are working with. It allows you to gather information about their prior experiences, and it allows them to reflect on what they want the purpose of these communities to be. The list you create as a team is also something you can come back to throughout the school year if things are getting off track. You can revisit the list and ask teachers in what ways the community is meeting or not meeting these goals and brainstorm ways to improve the community.

When I do this exercise with teams, I go one step further. After the discussion about the previous questions, I ask the team to draft a list of activities and products they would like to come out of our meetings. That way we have a coconstructed menu of items to work on when we meet. These menu items might include the following:

- Collaborating on lesson plans
- Looking at student work
- Doing a child study
- Creating assessments
- Interviewing students
- Discussing articles or books

Spending some time developing this list as a team sets a very different tone than when administrators tell teachers they are to "form professional learning communities," and then administrators dictate what teachers will do during this time. When administrators, teachers, and coaches work together as a team to coconstruct this list, I find the work becomes relevant and meaningful to all team members and has the greatest impact on students.

From my work in schools throughout the years, I really believe that if any change is going to be effective and enduring, it cannot be imposed on students, teachers, or families. These members need to be part of the decision-making. Whenever I hear an administrator say "teacher buy-in," I cringe. This phrase makes it seem as if we have to convince teachers to buy something we are selling them. In truth, we should all be part of creating that vision.

Jim Knight has written extensively on school change and the importance of shared leadership in effecting change. One of his suggestions is to offer teachers choices and value their voices. Giving them options of which practices will be implemented and how they will be implemented makes them more likely to take up new ideas (Knight 2009). The community-building activities described in this section were designed around the idea of creating an authentic shared space for members to learn together, with the end goal being to improve student learning. As you read through the activities, I encourage you to think about the learning communities you are trying to create, the relationships you are trying to build, and which activities might work best for your environment.

COMMUNITY-BUILDING ACTIVITIES

It can be tempting to get started right away with the activities you have coconstructed for your learning community (i.e., collaborating on lesson plans). However, I have found it's important to spend time on community-building activities first to set the tone for the work you will do as a team. When I initially started coaching, I began with a fun math brain teaser or puzzle, but I then realized that did not accomplish my goal of getting us to collaborate. These games also tended to be especially problematic when I worked with elementary school teachers or individuals with math anxiety. I began to look for activities that had an entry point for all and would create some fun and excitement around our work together. Just like I wanted my classroom to be a place of joy, I wanted teachers to feel a sense of joy when we worked together, so we needed a positive start. Yes, we were going to do serious work related to teaching and learning, but we needed to have some fun while doing it. I also wanted to choose activities that teachers could modify and use with their students, so that they would walk out of our session with something they could immediately bring back to their classrooms.

My goals are similar whether I am working with a group I have never met before or when I am trying to build community or reset norms with a group I already know. The goals I have for this work follow. You may want to add your own.

GOALS

- Setting or resetting norms for working together
- Creating opportunities to reflect on beliefs and attitudes toward teaching and learning math
- Getting to know each other
- Providing teachers with activities they can also use with their students
- Creating a positive, joyful environment

Although all the tasks that follow support the last three goals, I've found it's worthwhile to collect tasks that help me focus on the first two goals: setting or resetting norms and reflecting on beliefs and attitudes about math.

Setting or Resetting Norms for Working Together

The two activities in this section focus on developing or revisiting norms. I have found the first activity, the Marshmallow Challenge, works especially well with brand-new groups or when members have never worked with each other. For example, I use it sometimes when doing district-level professional development (PD) where teachers are from different schools and don't know one another. The second set of activities, the Complex Instruction Tasks—in particular, the Design Challenge—are useful when I need to reset norms. You may want to use them when a group you work with is starting to have some difficulties working together. They are also helpful when you are new to a group that has worked together before.

Marshmallow Challenge

The Marshmallow Challenge is one of my favorite activities to do with both adults and children. I've adapted it from Tom Wujec's work with teams across different organizations on how to collaborate and use design-thinking, which he described in a TED Talk (2010). This simple task is easy to prepare and facilitate, and it builds relationships among teacher teams.

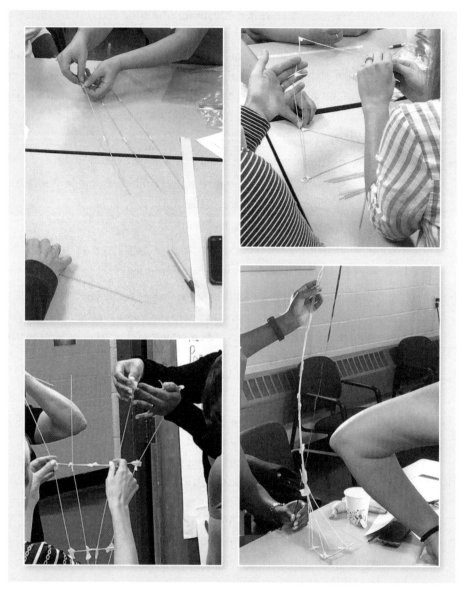

Figure 1.1
Teams working on the Marshmallow Challenge

Give each team of four a large sealable bag with the following items:

- 20 sticks of uncooked spaghetti
- 1 yard of masking tape
- 1 yard of string
- 1 marshmallow

Challenge the teams to use the materials to design the tallest freestanding structure in 18 minutes, following these rules:

- The goal is to build the tallest freestanding structure. The structure cannot be hung from a higher item.
- You can use all the items (except the sealable bag), or you can use some of them. You do not have to use all the items.
- You can cut or break the spaghetti, tape, and string.
- The marshmallow must be whole and on top. It cannot be cut!
- You must remove your hands from the structure as soon as time is over!

You can then set a visible timer for 18 minutes, turn on some music, and allow the groups to explore, as seen in Figure 1.1. This work time becomes a great opportunity for you to observe how members of the school work together. You might take notes on the following:

- Who takes a leadership role?
- Who is excited about the challenge?
- Who checks out?
- Who works well together?

If you collect this information during the activity, you can use it later to think about your work with the team and with individuals. Your notes can also help you think about strategic groupings and pairings.

After time is up, measure the structures and announce the winners. If your budget allows, a professional book is a nice prize. If not, a little token like a sticker, a piece of chocolate, or a certificate can work.

Although the actual activity is important, what is more valuable is the debrief after. I facilitate the conversation by posing the debrief questions listed here—you might want to use them, adapt them, or add questions of your own.

FACILITATION QUESTIONS for the
Marshmallow Challenge

? What was your role in the group? What did you contribute to the group that made the structure stronger?

? After seeing all the designs, how might you adjust your structure if you built a new one?

(continued)

> ❓ What would you do differently as an individual next time? What would you do differently as a group?
>
> ❓ How might you use this in your classroom? What might be the purpose for your students?
>
> ❓ What were the aspects of your team that allowed you to work well together? Not so well together?

I suggest you have everyone reflect and answer independently first, then discuss as a small group, and then share with the whole group. During the small-group discussions, you can circulate and listen in. This is a great chance to observe and gather information, so try to speak as little as possible.

After the whole group share-out, you might ask the team to think about the implications this activity has for your work together by posing an additional set of questions. Once again, you can ask them to reflect independently, then discuss in small groups, and then share with the whole class. Some questions I find helpful in facilitating the conversation follow.

FACILITATION QUESTIONS for Implications of the Marshmallow Challenge

> ❓ Based on this activity, what are some qualities you think are important for us to have as individuals when we are learning together as a team?
>
> ❓ What are some norms or structures you think we should create for our groups as we learn together?
>
> ❓ How did you address disagreements in the team? How might you use these strategies if we disagree in our work moving forward?

As groups share out, you can take notes, either on chart paper or electronically. Your role is to help colleagues come to a consensus about initial expectations and norms for working together. Here are some of the norms that have emerged when I have done this activity:

NORMS FOR WORKING TOGETHER

- Think outside the box! Because there was no single solution to the problem, we were able to tap into our creativity and try different ideas.
- Mistakes are valuable. We learned a lot from our designs that failed. They helped us modify the structures and create better ones.
- Our work as a group was stronger than our work would have been if we had worked independently.
- Different group members bring different contributions from their unique experiences and personalities. We learned interesting things about each other and how people thought about the task. So, although we may know things about how our colleagues teach, watching them engage in this task together showed us different aspects of their personalities.

It can be helpful to have a written record of these shared norms, which the team can come back to and modify as their work together progresses. It's important that these norms are grounded in a concrete experience that is shared together, rather than an abstract or hypothetical list. For example, when we create a norm like "Mistakes are valuable," we have a shared experience to connect it to. Team members often refer back to the experience, sometimes months or even years later: "This reminds me of when we made those marshmallow towers. When our first marshmallow structure collapsed, we figured

out the marshmallow was heavier than we thought and needed to be supported better with the base. Sometimes we just need to try things and see what happens." These shared experiences allow the list of norms to come alive and be meaningful and relevant to the work you will do together. If you want to know more about the Marshmallow Challenge, take a look at the resources on the 6 Tools website.

Complex Instruction Tasks

Sometimes groups need a chance to reset norms. For example, you may notice that team members aren't working well together anymore or that certain members are starting to feel uncomfortable having their classrooms visited by their peers. When this happens, it can be useful to take some time to revisit norms.

Elizabeth Cohen, Rachel Lotan, and their colleagues at the Stanford School of Education designed research-based activities with the goal of fostering equity by allowing opportunities for all students to be successful in heterogeneous classrooms. These "Complex Instruction" tasks, which have been studied with elementary, middle, and high school students, are designed to disrupt the hierarchies and unequal status that can occur when students work in groups. Although the activities are designed for teachers to use in their classrooms with students, I have found that they are easily adaptable to teacher teams and that facilitating them is a good way to reset norms.

The activities work nicely for teacher teams because group work can be just as difficult for teachers as it is for students. For example, one member of the group may dominate the conversation, or a member may feel that their ideas are not being heard. Sometimes it can be difficult to open ourselves to being vulnerable and taking risks in a group setting. Using these tasks has helped me bring some of these issues forward in a nonthreatening way so we can think about how to navigate them together. Although I use many of the activities from the Complex Instruction tasks, my favorite is an adaptation of their Master Designer activity. I call it the Design Challenge.

THE DESIGN CHALLENGE

GROUP SIZE: Four team members

MATERIALS:

- A set of geometric blocks for each team member. They must be exactly the same. I use either tangrams or pattern blocks.
- Dividers. I normally use two-pocket folders to create a divider between the members so that no one can see anyone else's workspace.
- A timer.

GOAL: To re-create the original design that one team member has created

RULES:

- A designer is randomly assigned. This person uses the shapes to create any design they want.
- After the designer has created their design, they explain how to create the design so that the other three team members can create the same image. They can use words, hand signals, and gestures.
- The team members can ask questions of the designer as well as of each other.

Figure 1.2
Teachers working on the Design Challenge

- ▨ When a group member thinks they have created the same design, the creator checks the design. If the member is correct, they are responsible for joining the designer in explaining how to create the design.

- ▨ The group is not done until all members are done with one design. If the group finishes and there is still time remaining, a new person takes on the role of the designer.

As the groups are working (as seen in Figure 1.2), you can circulate, observe, and take notes. The note-taking template provided in Appendix 1 and on the 6 Tools website may help you organize your observations.

When I facilitate, I try to record things I notice or comments I hear that might be helpful to discuss in the debrief. For example, I might record the confusion one team member was having about the orientation of the right triangle and how using more precise mathematical vocabulary (i.e., hypotenuse, legs) was helpful, but only for those members who were familiar with the vocabulary. I also might record the questions that team members asked that were productive ("Is it on your right or on my right?"). Sometimes team members will remember these specific comments, but it's helpful to have them written down in case they don't. You can see some more examples in Figure 1.3 on the following page. Alternatively, you could assign a fifth member to the group who does not participate directly in the task but instead records the questions asked. The fifth member can then share what they recorded with the group after the activity.

Design Challenge Note-Taking Template

GROUP 1	GROUP 2
Designer: Carolynn	Designer: Rasheema
Group Members: Emma, Jayson, Kamela	Group Members: Kat, Lena, Samantha
Notes: Jayson asked a lot of questions immediately.	Notes: Rasheema described the pattern using the names of the geometric shapes.
Emma was quiet and then mentioned she was stuck. Kamela asked her how they could help her.	Kat jumped in to help when Samantha mentioned she didn't remember which shape was the trapezoid.
Quotes: "Is it on my right or your right?"	Quotes: "Can someone repeat the last few steps? I got a little lost after we moved the trapezoid."
"Do you mean the hypotenuse or the leg of the triangle?"	"Lena, you haven't said anything. How are you doing?"

GROUP 3	GROUP 4
Designer: Patrick	Designer: Brenna
Group Members: Melissa, Shateema, Nicole	Group Members: Anna, Brian, Jasmine
Notes: Patrick gave step-by-step instructions to the group. Melissa asked clarifying questions about each step.	Notes: Brenna used hand signals to show the orientation of the shapes. Anna made the correct design and started helping to give directions.
Quotes: "The next step is to place the small triangle on the square."	Quotes: "Anna, can you help me give directions to the rest of the group?"
"Did you mean that we should place a small triangle on top of the square so that it looks like a little house?"	"To add to what Brenna said, the two large triangles are put together to make a large square."

Figure 1.3 Sample Design Challenge notes

While I circulate, I also look for the unique qualities of the individuals on the teams. What do they bring to the group? Who is a great communicator? Who observes first and thinks carefully before asking questions? Who asks interesting questions? These observations will help me think about how to build on strengths and strategically group our teams for later learning activities.

After the groups have completed the activity, I facilitate a discussion with the following questions. I use a similar format to the review of the Marshmallow Challenge, where members reflect independently first, then discuss in small groups, and then share out to the whole group.

FACILITATION QUESTIONS for the Design Challenge

? What was difficult about communicating in your group?

? What were some effective ways your group communicated?

? If you did this activity again with a new designer, what would you do differently?

During the whole-group discussion, I use my observation notes to strategically select which groups I would like to share out. This facilitation allows me to focus our discussion and also helps us address issues that team members might not necessarily volunteer or choose to share. For example, I might notice that one member of a group kept interrupting others and another group member asked them to let them finish their question. I might ask the group how they might navigate situations when a group member doesn't feel like they are being heard. If I noticed patterns in who spoke or didn't speak that seemed connected to race, gender, language, or disability, I might use that opportunity to open an important conversation. Or, I might take note for the moment and then do some careful planning about how to help the team explore their patterns and biases with an eye toward connecting these observations to discourse and status patterns among students.

After this share, we then go to a second set of questions. Depending on your situation, you may choose to have groups focus on one of these questions, some of them, or all of them. The goal is to leave the discussion and activity with an initial set of norms for communicating equitably within groups. As with the previous set of questions, the team reflects individually first, then in pairs or small groups, and then as a whole team.

FACILITATION QUESTIONS for Implications of the Design Challenge

❓ What can we do as a team to ensure all our group members are able to share their ideas?

❓ What are the implications of what we noticed during this activity for our communication as a group?

❓ What are some norms we can agree to as a group in terms of communication?

This activity allows us to begin a conversation about communication in our work together. It also allows me, as the coach, to assess what work will need to be done to continue the conversations. For example, after completing this activity, a teacher noted how having the shared goal of everyone creating the design helped her to stay engaged, even after she knew her design was correct. She liked that she then became a designer and helped give directions. I pushed the group to think about what that observation meant for our work as teachers as well as for our work as learners together. We came up with a shared norm that when we worked in teams, our goal was to make sure that we all understood the content or the details of a particular teacher strategy before we moved on, and that it was everyone's responsibility to help one another understand new content or strategies. If you want to know more about other Complex Instruction tasks, take a look at the 6 Tools website.

Creating Opportunities to Reflect on Beliefs and Attitudes Toward Teaching and Learning Math

I have found these next activities helpful in allowing me to assess team member's beliefs and attitudes toward doing math, learning math, and teaching math. They also create a space for team members to reflect on their experiences and share these reflections with each other. If possible, I try to do these exercises after some initial team-building work, such as the activities described earlier, because it can be scary to share personal beliefs and attitudes. Having norms already established can make the work more productive. Knowing your group, you can tailor the activities in a way that makes everyone comfortable.

Four Corners

Whenever I tell people what I do for a living, they respond in extreme ways. On one hand I hear:

"I've always been great at math."

"I used to be the fastest at my multiplication tables. I loved winning those contests."

"I loved finding x."

"I loved that there was only one answer."

"I had a teacher that did the coolest math projects with us."

On the other hand, I also hear:

"I hate math."

"I'm not a math person."

"I had a third-grade teacher who told me I would never be good at math."

"I hated math. Ms. Smith quizzed us on multiplication facts in front of the class, and I forgot mine."

"I liked math until we got to fractions (or algebra or calculus)."

After countless conversations, I began to realize that everyone has a math story. We've created narratives for ourselves about our relationships to math, and many times they were influenced greatly by our experiences in school. Our stories often contain positive parts: sometimes we think of a math teacher who didn't give up on us or a project that showed us that math could be fun and relates to our lives. But there can also be negative parts: the time when math stopped making sense to us, or the time we felt we weren't good at math because we couldn't answer 7 x 6 fast enough. It's important for us to reflect on our experiences with math and how they affect us as teachers. As a coach, it's valuable for me to hear these stories from the teachers I will be working with. It's also valuable for the teachers to share and hear one another's stories so they can learn more about each other's backgrounds and experiences with math. This exercise may seem most important for our teachers who had negative experiences with math, but it is equally critical for those who had positive experiences. For example, if people say they are "good" at math and that math came "naturally" to them, I ask them to reflect on what "good" or "natural" at math means and to consider implications for how they view their students' abilities and potential.

One way to have teachers begin this work on their beliefs about math is to ask them to reflect on their most *vivid* memory of being a math student. What do they remember most about being a student in a K–12 math classroom? They shouldn't overthink it; they should write down the first memory that comes to mind. I'll share mine:

> *When I was in fourth grade, I remember the teacher assigning the number of the problems we needed to complete on our own. I would finish them quickly, and the teacher would then ask me to check the work of other kids and help them. I was shy and didn't want any attention drawn to me, so I started working really slowly so I wouldn't have to help anyone.*

STOP and JOT

 Take a minute to think about your experiences with math as a student. What's the first memory that comes to mind?

With your teachers, after a brief time to think, ask them to jot their memory on an index card. Once they've done this, you can begin the Four Corners activity. Mark each corner of the room with one of the following labels:

- Strongly agree
- Agree
- Disagree
- Strongly disagree

You can then read a statement such as, "Some people are math people," or "I learned why rules worked in math class." Individuals take their index card with them and go to the corner that reflects how they feel about the statement. In the corner, they find a partner, share their memories, and then talk about why they picked that corner. Each time you share a new statement, teachers move and find a new partner to talk with. Here are some statements I have found useful for this activity:

- I love doing math problems.
- Math class was a positive experience for me in elementary school.
- Math class was a positive experience for me in middle school.
- Some people are math people.
- Math is my favorite subject to teach (for elementary school teachers).
- A lot of discussion occurred in my math class when I was a student.
- My math teachers encouraged boys to participate more often in math class.
- I learned why rules worked in my math classes.
- Math is best done independently.
- Students of all racial and ethnic backgrounds had equal opportunities in math classes when I was in school.
- I get frustrated if I can't solve a problem immediately.
- Doing math is fun.
- I feel anxious when I am asked to solve a math problem.
- Math is a universal language.

You may want to add other statements. One resource to use for additional statements is Shelia Tobias's math anxiety questionnaire from her book *Overcoming Math Anxiety* (1993). The book is also a nice resource to use if your group wants to dive deeper into the topic of math anxiety.

The purpose of using these statements is to discuss our attitudes toward doing math, our experiences learning math, and our experiences teaching math. After reviewing several of these statements, you can come back as a whole group and debrief using the following questions.

FACILITATION QUESTIONS for Four Corners

- How do our experiences as learners shape the way we teach math?
- How do our beliefs and attitudes about math affect the way our students perceive math?
- How did our race, gender, sexuality, language, and/or disability status impact our experiences in math classes? How do they affect our students?
- What are some ways we try to help students have positive experiences with math? What do we struggle with?
- What are some questions related to this discussion that we want to learn more about as a group? What research might we want to explore?

Reflecting on and talking about our experiences allows us to think about the instructional decisions we make. For example, because of my experience of being a student who finished work early, I see myself in those students in my class, and I think about ways to challenge them differently than I would if I didn't have that experience. However, I may miss these opportunities for students who were not like me. Talking with teachers who had opposite backgrounds—maybe they were the students who struggled—allows me to begin to understand that perspective. Having these discussions as a group allows us to process some of our experiences so that we can be aware of how they influence our teaching, both positively and negatively.

The questions about equity allow us to have conversations about our identities and our students' identities and how they come into play in the math classroom. We have all had different experiences based on who we are, and it can be important to learn more about them. For example, I often share my time of being in graduate-level math courses with mostly men, and how I was sometimes dismissed and ignored by male professors. These statements can open conversations about the different opportunities others in the group have been given or denied based on their gender or race or ethnicity or home language. In addition, hearing about our team members' lived experiences can springboard a conversation about our students and how their identities may impact their own achievement in the classroom.

The last question on the debrief list allows us to share resources and provide readings for the group. For example, math anxiety is a topic that often comes up, and the group may want to learn more about how to address it, including what support might be available for families. In future meetings, we can explore different research and resources on the topic, such as Sheila Tobias's book. In my experience, this process creates a different culture than if I immediately shared the resources or told the team that this is the topic we will explore in meetings. Instead, I created an experience where this topic naturally arises and becomes of interest to the group, and, therefore, the learning is more self-directed.

Chalk Talk—Assessing Teaching Beliefs and Attitudes

After we have had a chance to process our experiences and identities as learners, it's important to learn more about the team's beliefs about what it means to do math, learn math, and teach math. I use the following activity to gather information. As you imagine facilitating it, make sure to think about how you'd answer as well.

STOP and JOT

 Close your eyes. Think of your favorite math lesson you taught this year or last year. Picture the room. What are the students saying? What would I hear if I walked into the room? What would I see? What are the students doing? What are you doing? Open your eyes and jot down some notes if you need.

I wonder what you thought about when you pictured your favorite math lesson. I have several lessons that come to mind from my time teaching, and it's a joy to reflect on them. I also wonder how you anticipate the teachers you work with will answer this question, and what glimpses you'll get into the many wonderful things that are going on in classrooms. When facilitating this activity with a team, you will want to give them about 5–10 minutes to reflect and jot down some notes before you introduce the idea of a chalk talk to the group. When you introduce chalk talk for the first time, it is helpful to go over the following directions:

- Each person has a marker.
- There is *no* talking until time is up.
- Try to write something on each poster.
- Put a check mark if you agree.
- Write a question if you don't understand what someone wrote.
- Answer any questions that people have written.

Hang chart paper around the room with the following questions, pass out markers, and invite people to begin the chalk talk:

- What did the math classroom you described look like?
- What did the math classroom you described sound like?
- Why did you choose this lesson as your favorite lesson?
- What are some of the obstacles that prevent you from having lessons that are engaging all the time?

After about ten quiet minutes (depending on the size of the group), split the group so some members are at each poster, and then invite them to talk. Their goal is to look for patterns in the responses to their question and summarize the poster for the whole group.

While they talk, you can circulate and assess what they believe a good math lesson is. You can also ask probing questions to help facilitate the conversations and push for more specific responses. For example, a response might be that students were engaged "in a hands-on lesson." I might ask the small group if all hands-on lessons are cognitively engaging and then push them to go deeper and be more specific about what it was about those particular hands-on lessons that pushed student thinking.

I've done this activity many times, and I've rarely had anyone say that their favorite lesson is one where the kids sat and worked on a textbook page or a set of similar problems. The lessons they share are usually hands-on, involve rich tasks, are project-based, and engage students. Sharing these experiences and examining the patterns that emerge allow for the group to create a shared vision of what they want math classrooms to look like—a vision that grows from

33

the positive experiences they have had when trying different types of student-centered activities. This coconstructed vision will help us as we begin to plan lessons together and visit each other's classrooms. Focusing on these experiences from the students' perspectives by asking what the students were doing and saying during the activity allows us to ignore, for a little bit at least, the challenges of planning and implementing these types of lessons regularly. For now, the goal is for the group to begin coming to a consensus on their goals and vision. As the coach, you'll be able to help them get there in your work together. You might even save the charts or take pictures of them so that when you are engaged in learning walks or lesson study, you'll have some anchoring ideas to come back to as you begin working toward your shared vision.

Finally, the chalk talk and discussion create positive energy and honor the work that teachers do. Thinking about our favorite lessons and celebrating them with one another makes everyone feel good. Every teacher can think of one great lesson and feel successful, which leads to a positive conversation that helps everyone get to know one another as teachers. We can learn about each other's teacher magic and start to get a glimpse inside one another's classrooms, which lays the groundwork for the in-person visits to come.

Reflecting on Our Beliefs and Attitudes Toward Coaching

Many teachers will have had prior experiences with coaching, both positive and negative. It can be helpful to allow teachers to reflect on these experiences and think about how they prefer to learn and grow as professionals. One way to do this is by having the group respond to the following questions individually:

- What coaching/feedback experiences have been the most positive for you? Why?
- What coaching/feedback experiences have been challenging for you? Why?

It can be helpful to have the teachers record this somewhere visible—either on chart paper or on an online tool like Padlet, which allows them to see their colleagues' experiences and gives you a record to reference.

After giving the group time to share their experiences with one another, I find it helpful to share an outside perspective on coaching and professional learning. To do this, we either watch a portion of Atul Gawande's TED Talk: "Want to Get Great at Something? Get a Coach," or read his article "Personal Best" (2011). Dr. Gawande is a surgeon who talks about his reluctance to have a coach come into his operating room and then goes on to share what he learned from the experience. He also details the role of coaching in other fields, like sports and music. I've found that thinking about how other professions use coaches can shift our perceptions about coaching and also push our thinking about how professionals continue to learn and grow.

After watching the video or reading the article, pose the following reflection questions.

FACILITATION QUESTIONS for Coaching Discussion

- Do you agree with the idea that everyone needs a coach? Why or why not?
- How does this video/article connect with your own experiences with coaching or receiving feedback?

Ask team members to reflect independently, and then share in small groups, and then share with the whole group. As facilitator, you can summarize the conversation by asking the group to think about how they would like to move forward in your work as a group and what they are looking for in a coach and from the coaching experience.

This activity allows you to get to know more about the group you are working with and what their coaching experiences have been in the past so that you have important context for your work. It also allows you to frame coaching in a positive light and begin to create a shared vision of why professional learning is important for all members of a team.

IMPLEMENTING THE ACTIVITIES: QUESTIONS AND CHALLENGES

Now that we've looked at some different activities that can be used to build community with a group, let's explore some of the questions and challenges that might arise when you begin to plan how you will put these activities into practice.

Implementation Questions

As you reflect on how to use these tasks with your teacher teams, think about which tasks would work best for your group. There is no right way to choose which tasks to implement, and your context may dictate some of the ways in which you modify the activities. Although situations vary, I've noticed the questions in the next sections are common among most coaches.

When Do We Do These Activities?

I've shared some ways I've built and sustained effective learning communities because I believe that building relationships is fundamental to coaching. Often, I get pushback that there isn't enough time to spend doing activities like these, and time is certainly precious. However, I strongly believe that if the time is not spent to build a strong community at the start, the rest of the work will not be as impactful. For example, I don't find it useful to begin a learning walk with a group of people unless I have had some time to set norms. That said, I've often shortened some of the previous activities so that I can be respectful of everyone's time. I've also weaved them throughout my work with a group. For example, we might do a Complex Instruction activity at the start of each month's meeting to revisit how we work together. I encourage you to think flexibly about when you might use these activities in your context. Although it's great to have a big chunk of time, it's not necessary to have an in-service or early-release day to open these conversations.

What's the Role of Administrators?

I've done these activities with administrators participating as team members. I've done them without administrators being in the room at all. And I've done this work with teams of administrators, where no teachers were present. Each model serves a different purpose with no one right answer. Removing the administrators from the room can allow for a more honest conversation, so I use this technique when I know that teachers need a safe space to talk about their identities and experiences with math. I've used these activities with just administrators for a similar reason. Sometimes they need to feel that they are in a safe space to admit some of their insecurities and experiences with math. They may not yet feel that they can be vulnerable in front of their teams. My ultimate goal, however, is for us all to be in the same room, participating equally, which means that administrators should share their experiences as well, rather than sit in the room, observing. I've found that when everyone is vulnerable enough to participate, we can really begin to make movement forward as learners together.

For example, a principal I worked with was frustrated with her K–2 team. She told me that they were successful and creative when teaching reading and writing, but they were completely different teachers when she observed them teaching math. I suggested she do the Four Corners activity with them. After she did the activity during a faculty meeting, she told me, "I had no idea how they felt about math. They have some real anxiety related to it. Almost all of them went to the strongly disagree or disagree corner for 'Math class was a positive experience for me in elementary school.' They told me stories of how a teacher embarrassed them or how math stopped making sense to them at a certain point. I felt terrible listening to their stories. I feel like I understand them differently now." This activity was instrumental for that team to begin making changes. Having the principal share her experiences (she had positive experiences in math and loved it as student and teacher) and having the teachers share theirs provided a chance for both to see things from one another's perspective.

Implementation Challenges

Just like we anticipate and plan for different student responses during a math lesson, we need to anticipate and plan for different responses we might get during these activities.

STOP and JOT

 Take a minute to think about and jot what challenges you might face in implementing any of the activities described earlier.

I'm going to share the two most common challenges I face. My guess is that they are similar to ones you just wrote down.

What Do I Do About the Nonparticipator?

Ms. A doesn't want to share or participate. I've been told (or I've seen) her do amazing things in her classroom. She has a lot of knowledge and experience that the group would benefit from. However, she prefers to work alone and, as a result, often shuts down during any group tasks.

I relate to this scenario because this was how I behaved often as a teacher. I checked out during professional development group activities. I especially hated when the coach or administrator would single me out and ask me to share with the group something I did. (If you go back to my most vivid memory of being a math student, this reaction should make sense to you.) As a result, when I see this behavior as a coach, I can understand it.

The way I address nonparticipation is to appeal to the idea that all of the students in the school or district are our students, and so we need to share our ideas so that all of them can benefit. I also try to use activities where all members are responsible for the task. The Designer Challenge described earlier is great for emphasizing the importance of each member working together. I also use activities from Tim Erickson's books *United We Solve* (1995) and *Get It Together* (1989), where each member has a clue but cannot share their clue with the rest of the team. This structure forces all members to be involved.

I also think carefully about strategic grouping and the roles of the members. Sometimes I'll assign roles and ask a teacher like Ms. A to be the recorder in the group or to be the one that shares out. This responsibility will actively involve her in a specific part of the task, but she might feel more comfortable sharing other people's work at first. My goal is that over time she'll start to share her own ideas as she is charting or recording ideas from the group.

What Do I Do About the "This Won't Work" Participant?

Ms. B finds something wrong with every activity. She says things like, "My students would take the spaghetti and throw it at one another." As a result, she doesn't engage with the activities and can derail the team-building aspects of the activities by sometimes behaving as she believes her students would.

Teachers who derail activities or discussions with comments about why "this won't work" might be talking about a specific activity, like the Marshmallow Challenge, or about a more general idea about teaching, like using manipulatives. They also may approach the activities with a deficit mindset and say things like, "Our kids can't do this." When I encounter this type of resistance, I think about my philosophy about learning: I believe that people construct their own understanding by doing and engaging. So, sometimes these teachers need to engage in the activity themselves as learners, and other times, they need an opportunity to see these activities in action in their own classroom.

When I encounter this type of participant, I try several things. One tactic is to ask them to suspend disbelief and do a thought experiment with me. I might say, "I know there are many challenges with modifying this for your class, but let's table those for a moment and just pretend that this is happening in a different class, and everything is going smoothly. Let's talk about the activity for what it is and what potential it might have. You can jot down any concerns you anticipate, and we will come back to the challenges at the end." Sometimes I will use a parking lot poster so I can collect the group's thoughts all together; other times, I'll have them write their own notes. I always make sure to come back to their concerns at the end, although by that point, they sometimes aren't as pressing. I often present the challenges to the group and have them brainstorm solutions before I give any suggestions. For example, when Ms. B says her students are going to throw the marshmallows, I legitimize the concern and then turn to the group and ask what they suggest. If they don't have any ideas, I'll share something I saw another teacher do.

Another tactic is to volunteer to coplan and coteach the activity in Ms. B's classroom, which aligns nicely with my belief of learning as doing. Instead of us talking about what we think students might do, we do the activity and talk about what really happens. You will have to figure out the logistics of this move, but it often is my go-to response when working with this type of teacher. Sometimes, I have stopped in the middle of PD and gone into a classroom to try out an idea. Other times, I have suggested lesson study, which we will talk about in Tool 6. Sometimes, I pull students into a meeting and do a student interview with them, which we will talk about next, in Tool 2. All of these moves allow teachers to see things in action with students, which pushes the conversation away from hypotheticals and gives us data with the students in our school to discuss. Attitudes will not change overnight, but this tactic does allow the conversation to shift. I've heard teachers begin to say things like, "I don't think they can do that problem, but let's grab some kids and ask them to try it," which is a great first step.

We will continue to discuss challenges we face in our coaching and how to address them as we explore the different coaching tools. They all allow us to build on the relationships we are cultivating. Before we get into the work of being in one another's classrooms and trying out new ideas and taking risks, we need to build trust and the idea that we are learning together. Furthermore, shifting focus to our students is so important and needs to happen before we give feedback on teaching practices. If we start with giving feedback on teaching, teachers can get defensive and feel that their teaching is being evaluated. If we focus on students, we can move student learning to the forefront. We can then think about how teaching impacts learning. This is why I suggest introducing student interviews as an early step in your coaching work. We'll jump into interviews next, but first, take some time to reflect.

REFLECTING on LEARNING

- Think about the group you currently work with or will be working with. Which of the activities would you like to try with them first? Why? What are your goals for the activity? How will you know whether you are successful?

- Think about your most successful coaching experience or relationship. What made it successful? How can you build on that in your future work?

- Think about your most unsuccessful coaching experience or relationship. What made it unsuccessful? What did you learn from that experience that will influence your work moving forward?

- I shared two types of challenging participants that you might encounter. What other challenges do you anticipate? How might you address them?

EXPLORING the LITERATURE

Research supports the idea that creating community is an important part of professional learning (Brodie 2013; Borko 2004; Darling-Hammond et al. 2017; Desimone 2009; Franke and Kazemi 2001; Grossman et al. 2001; Vescio et al. 2008). According to the literature, successful communities are:

- Ongoing
- Reflective
- Collaborative
- Inclusive
- Learning-oriented

The work that I have found most interesting and that has guided the development of many of the activities I shared in this section is by Grossman, Wineburg, and

Woolworth (2001). They studied teacher learning and developed a theory about how to create professional learning communities that were safe, sustainable, collaborative, and high-functioning. The four steps they propose to help develop communities are:

1 Form a group identity and norms of interaction.

2 Navigate differences among group members.

3 Negotiate the tensions between the goals of improving professional practice and fostering intellectual development.

4 Foster communal responsibility for individual growth.

In addition, the authors identified features of successful professional learning communities, such as safe communities where teachers feel comfortable being vulnerable, sharing ideas, and engaging in productive struggle without judgment. They also talk about the need to listen actively to one another and understand one another's perspectives.

STUDENT INTERVIEWS
Learning to Listen

Tyson, a second-grade student, sits in the middle of our grade-level team meeting with a math problem in front of him. The team had selected the problem from a recent assessment because more than three-quarters of the class struggled with it.

"Hi Tyson," I say. "Thanks for sitting with us today. We are going to ask you to do a couple of math problems with us. While you work, we would love it if you could think out loud and tell us what's going on in your head. We are really curious about how you solve the problem. Does that sound OK to you?"

"Sure." Tyson looks around at all of us.

"Let's start with you reading the problem to us."

An art museum has 658 paintings. The museum also has 569 drawings. How many more paintings than drawings does the museum have?

Tyson circles 658, 569, and "more" on his paper. He then writes 658 + 569.

"Can you tell us what you are thinking?" I ask. "Why did you write 658 + 569?"

"Oh. Am I wrong?"

"I don't know. I'm just curious why you wrote it. When I ask you why you did something, it doesn't necessarily mean it's right or wrong. I am just trying to see inside your brain and understand what you are thinking."

"OK. I saw the word 'more,' and I know that the word 'more' means that you add, so I added the two numbers that I circled."

The teachers look around at each other. This same thing happened with two students in earlier interviews. They told us how they looked for the "key words" when they solved problems.

"Tyson, thanks so much for sharing your thinking with us today. We learned so much from you." I lead Tyson out of the room and then bring in a student who solved the problem correctly. She doesn't rely on key words. Instead, she shares an interesting mental math strategy.

"OK. You have a group of paintings and a group of drawings. And you have more paintings than drawings, but you want to know how many more. So, basically, you want to know what plus 569 will equal 658. So, I added 100 and that gave me 669 and then took away 11 to get to 658, so I needed to subtract the 11 from 100 so it is 89. There are 89 more paintings than drawings."

During the interviews, the teachers listen and take notes. We also video-tape the interviews so that we can go back to them if we need to. After the interviews are completed, we debrief as a team. We discuss what we notice about what students are thinking.

"I feel like I've been teaching these key words as a support, but I'm not sure they are helping," Ms. Richards says.

"The student who solved the problem correctly used some interesting mental math strategies. I wonder why she used a missing-addend problem instead of writing a subtraction problem," Mr. Blythe adds.

"Can you say a little more about that? What could be some reasons she did that?" I pose to the group.

After talking about why the student used adding up to solve the problem, I ask about our next steps. "So, if we are finding key words problematic, what other teaching strategies can we try to help students solve word problems? How can we get students to stop relying on key words? Maybe we can think about that and then discuss it in our next meeting." As we wrap up the team meeting, we make a note to explore different problem-solving strategies in our next meeting.

HOW CAN WE DEVELOP OUR COACHING SKILLS THROUGH STUDENT INTERVIEWS?

I started to use student interviews in my coaching work when I reflected on the experiences that transformed my teaching. The way I taught changed significantly when I began listening to students with the goal of *making sense of what they were doing*. Previously, I listened for assessment purposes: did the student get it right? Did they get it wrong? If they got it wrong, how was I going to help them get it right? With the best of intentions, I focused on what part they got wrong and then immediately tried to make sure all students got to the correct solution. As a result, however, I often asked students leading questions that dragged them to the correct answer rather than making sense of their thinking. I missed so much. I wasn't hearing all the interesting ways students thought about the problem, and I misunderstood their ideas.

As an example, I often saw students solving fraction problems this way:

$$\frac{1}{3} + \frac{1}{4} = \frac{2}{7}$$

If you have worked with students on fractions, you have probably seen this thinking as well. I knew that students were adding the numerators and the denominators and assumed it was because they didn't realize the pieces weren't the same size. As a result, I tried to remediate by leading them to the solution.

Me (pointing to the two fractions): I see you added the numerators and denominators. Are those pieces the same size?

Student (looking confused): Yes.

Me: Are you *sure* those pieces are the same size?

Student: Um. No.

Me: Good! So, what do we do if they aren't the same size?

Student: Um . . .

Me: I'll give you a hint. We worked on it yesterday. We need to find . . .

Student: The same size?

Me: Yes. We need to find common . . .

Student: Umm . . . denominators?

Me: Yes. Very good! We need to find common denominators. Why don't you review your notes from yesterday or look at the anchor chart on how to find the common denominator and then redo this?

When I was working with students like this, I truly believed that with some prompting or a hint, they would remember what to do. I didn't understand that I was dragging them through a solution path that made sense to me. They were playing the game and following along with me based on what they thought I wanted them to say. Eventually, I realized learning wasn't occurring with all my prompting, and I needed to change my approach. I tried to figure out *why* students were solving the problem in different ways than how I anticipated they would solve it.

Me: Can you tell me how you got your answer?

Student: Is it wrong?

Me: I don't know. Why don't you explain it to me, and we will try to figure it out.

Student: Well, here you have one out of three things (pointing to one-third), and here you are adding one out of four things (pointing to one-fourth), so basically you now have two out of seven things (pointing to two-sevenths).

Me: Interesting. Can you try using these fraction strips/number line/fraction circles to show me another way to solve it?

When I started asking questions to make sense of what students were doing and thinking, it was eye-opening. I could see how this solution made sense to students if they thought of a fraction as two, distinct, whole numbers and not as a number itself. Listening to students' thinking made me rethink the "out of" fraction language I was using, and whether I was sufficiently allowing students to explore a variety of models. I also revisited activities that explored the concept of fractions as a number before I tried to address the addition of fractions.

Most importantly, this line of questioning helped me change my responses to students. Instead of giving students a hint or reminding them of what we had done the day before, my response was to learn more about how they were thinking, whether or not they got the problem correct. I became fascinated by all the ways students thought about problems.

When I started coaching, I noticed that many of my math teachers were having the same trouble when listening to students. I thought about what tools I could use to really help them develop their listening skills and get them curious about student thinking. Visiting classrooms is one way to do this (and we'll talk about that in Tool 3: Visiting Classrooms), but I found that student interviews were also an effective way to begin this work.

Interviewing students as a team takes the focus off teaching and puts it on students' thinking—not completely, of course, because we need to choose tasks and tools available to the students. However, the goal of the interaction is not to teach the students a new concept but to observe how they think. I've found that the more we do these interviews, the more teachers become better observers of and listeners to student thinking in their classrooms.

INTERVIEWING STUDENTS AS A COACHING TOOL

Student interviews can be powerful tools in our coaching toolboxes. They allow us to focus on student thinking and have interesting conversations about how students solve different problems. They also allow us to develop our listening and questioning skills.

Goals of Student Interviews

My goals when using student interviews in my coaching work follow:

- To strengthen our listening skills
- To analyze what students are doing and why
- To increase our curiosity about student thinking
- To develop our questioning skills
- To develop our understanding of different mathematical strategies
- To focus our attention on what students *can* do

STOP and JOT

 Think for a minute about the teachers you work with and how they listen and respond to students in their classroom. What strengths and challenges do you see during classroom conversations, small-group work, or one-on-one interactions?

When I reflected on the teachers I work with, I found many of the following strengths:

- Building relationships with students
- Giving feedback to students
- Circulating and listening to student conversations
- Asking students to explain their work
- Encouraging students to discuss strategies with one another
- Selecting students to share with the whole group
- Asking students to agree and disagree with strategies presented

I also noticed the following challenges:

- Listening only for the right answer
- Listening only for a particular solution path
- Thinking about their next instructional move instead of listening to the response being given
- Assuming that students are thinking the same ways we are thinking
- Asking leading questions
- Not giving enough wait time for students to think about the problem
- Not allowing students to finish their thoughts because of an assumption about their thinking
- Listening for what students *don't* know instead of what they *do know*

- Questioning only the students who have incorrect answers
- Making assumptions about students' understanding based on characteristics like gender, home language, disabilities, and so on
- Not listening for the informal knowledge students bring to the problem

These challenges are understandable! It's hard to listen and respond to students in the moment in the classroom. As teachers, we have many things to pay attention to, and sometimes analyzing and responding to students' thinking in the moment is difficult.

You might consider having an explicit conversation with your team about these challenges and the importance of listening to students' thinking. During your team meeting, perhaps ask teachers to reflect on the prompt in the previous Stop and Jot. You can respond as well, so your colleagues understand that you too have encountered similar difficulties.

Sharing these challenges can help you frame student interviews as a solution. Interviews are one way we can develop and practice these skills of listening and responding to students.

Benefits of "Asking a Kid"

After a few rounds of team-interviewing students during meetings or PD time, you'll hopefully begin to hear teachers say, "Let's ask a kid," especially if your team is struggling with thinking about a task or an assessment. This is a great development, because it means teachers are expressing curiosity about students' thinking and beginning to see the benefits of interviews in their teacher toolboxes. Interviews help us center student thinking and dig into the mathematics. They also allow us to gather data about anticipated strategies, which are important parts of planning.

I also use interviews as a coaching strategy when I hear someone say, "My kids can't do that." Instead of getting into a discussion about what we believe children might do, I bring some students into the room to get data about what's possible. "Asking a kid" becomes a powerful tool for changing the way we view and approach planning and instruction because it forces us to question some of our assumptions and expectations.

Another unexpected benefit of interviews is that they can change the mood of meetings. Sometimes teams talk negatively about students and the way they learn. When we bring a student into the room, we cannot engage in this dialogue, obviously. And students really lighten teachers' moods! We all become engaged and interested in that child. Looking at student work and watching videos are great, but they do not yield quite the same power as having an authentic conversation with a young person from our school.

Finally, bringing students in creates an atmosphere of "Let's just try it. We'll see what happens." The interviews allow us to take risks that we might not be as comfortable taking in a classroom. Asking one student to solve a difficult task or use manipulatives is a baby step into trying this move with a whole class.

STUDENT INTERVIEWS IN ACTION

How do we get started? During an interview in a team meeting or PD, we present a task to a student and then encourage the student to think aloud while performing the task. One of the team members asks probing questions to uncover more about what the student is thinking (and help us develop our questioning skills). At the end of the interview, we analyze the data we collected (the student's responses, the student's work) and come up with some theories about what they were thinking, as well as some next steps, which we record so we can revisit them later. Although we focus on only a handful of students, what we learn is often generalizable to other students, so we discuss next steps for the class as a whole.

Student interviews are a flexible tool, and I've used them in several ways with different schools. You may want to consider using the following steps to roll out student interviews, but feel free to skip some and/or modify others. You also may want to develop your own interviewing skills first, perhaps with another coach.

STEP 1 Introducing student interviews to the team

STEP 2 Selecting tasks

STEP 3 Practicing the interview

STEP 4 Selecting students

STEP 5 Conducting the interviews

STEP 6 Analyzing the interviews

As you read through the specifics of each of these steps, you may find the Student Interview Planning Template to be helpful. You can find it in Appendix 2

and on the 6 Tools website. I use it to sketch out my learning plan for the team before I begin the work. As with a lesson plan for students, the team often modifies the plan based on needs and context. However, creating the initial learning plan allows me to be clear on my goals and plan at the start of the work. You may find it helpful to jot ideas on it as you read through the different steps.

STEP 1 Introducing Student Interviews to the Team

Ideally, the need to do interviews will come out of a particular problem that arises in a team meeting or in one of the relationship-building activities from our previous chapter. For example, when getting to know your teams, you may find that teachers notice students are struggling with specific mathematical topics. This organic discussion offers a great opportunity to set up interviews around those topics. Or, in your initial meetings with teachers, you might hear, "My kids can't do that." "That" can refer to rigorous tasks in the curriculum, standards-based questions, or mental math. You might use these tasks as a starting point for student interviews, so the team can investigate what students *can* do. Similarly, if the team is looking at an article or book and is curious or skeptical about the teaching strategy, you can design interviews in response.

For example, one team I worked with was studying Number Talks. We had read an article and watched some of the videos from *Number Talks* (Parrish 2022a and 2022b). However, teachers were afraid that their classes wouldn't have any strategies to solve the problem 16 x 25. Having done this type of problem with students many times, I knew they would have multiple strategies, but I also knew that me telling the teachers that students could do it would not convince them. I asked the team to choose three students to interview. In this case, two students were able to solve the problem with two different strategies, and one student got stuck. We learned a lot from all three of them. More importantly, the conversation shifted from what students *can't do* to what they *can do*.

If the need does not arise organically, you can introduce the idea of student interviews first, and then teachers can decide how the interviews could be useful in their work. It's essential that colleagues see these interviews as relevant to them. One of the mistakes I made early on in coaching was forgetting that teachers needed to see the need for any tool we used in professional development. I would get so excited about a new idea and forget that everyone needed to go through their own journey to be just as excited as I was. Therefore, the process would result in the teachers either resisting or complying, but rarely was it as beneficial as when they saw the relevance for themselves and chose to be active participants.

I think often about my reaction to new ideas presented to me as a teacher. I hated when I felt that a new initiative or idea was being forced on me by the administration or coaches, even if the idea might have been good. However, I loved learning about new things I thought would help me with something I was working on. For example, I knew my students were struggling with simple computation skills, but I didn't know what to do. When I learned about Number Talks, I was so happy to find something to try. But if Number Talks had been forced upon me, I'm not sure I would have been as receptive.

I often hear from administrators and coaches that they get a lot of resistance to professional development and to change and to new initiatives. I really believe that the majority of teachers are not opposed to change and are constantly looking for ways to learn. Just go on Twitter or look at the popularity of different blogs or count the number of teachers that use their own funding to go to conferences or buy resources online. It's not that teachers don't want to learn about new things; rather, it's the forced delivery of the new ideas to which they're opposed. So, when we introduce interviews, we should introduce them as a tool, discuss what might be some appropriate goals for using them, and talk about how we think this tool will help us help our students. If the tool turns out to not be helpful to our goal of serving students, we don't have to use it anymore. We can find another tool that helps us learn more about our students and how they think so that we can best foster learning. Continuing to come back to the centrality of serving our students is important when introducing and using any tool.

In addition to honoring authentic needs and being transparent when introducing a new professional development tool, I've found it can be helpful to ground any new tool in a reading. This text becomes something we can all refer to, and the idea becomes one that we are all trying, myself included. Bringing in an outside author makes it clear that interviews (or any other new tool) are not *my* idea or something I, or the admins, are pushing on anyone. They are tools or strategies that we are all learning about together because other educators have found them useful. We can then discuss the affordances and limitations of the idea together. Reading professional journals and discussing recent research together also fosters the culture of learning that we want to encourage at our schools.

For student interviews, here are some suggestions for readings to use with your teams:

■ If you want to do a book study, *Children's Mathematics: Cognitively Guided Instruction* (2014) by Carpenter et al. is a great place to start. You could also choose salient chapters if you do not have time for the entire book.

■ If you want to introduce the work with some shorter articles, I recommend the two below:

● Kazemi, Gibbons, Lomax, and Franke's "Listening to and Learning from Student Thinking" (2016).

● Buschman's "Using Student Interviews to Guide Classroom Instruction: An Action Research Project" (2001).

After reading the article or excerpt, you might pose the following questions for discussion.

FACILITATION QUESTIONS for Articles
About Student Interviews

❓ What are the important characteristics of student interviews?

❓ How are interviews different from observing a student in your class?

❓ What questions do you have about how to conduct interviews?

❓ How do you see them helping us in our work?

As you facilitate the conversation, capture the growing consensus on chart paper or a shared document. The following list of main points might help you get started.

■ Interviews are used to gather information about how a student is *thinking*.

■ Interviews are not designed to be teaching sessions; rather, they are designed to help us gather as much information as possible about student thinking.

■ Interviews require flexible questioning to determine what the student is thinking.

- Our goal is to make sense of the student's thinking and assume that what the student is doing makes sense to them.

- At the end, we want to try to make some generalizations and next steps for our work.

STEP 2 Selecting Tasks

As in the classroom, task selection is really important for interviews. We want to use a task that will tell us something we want to know more about. Depending on our goal, we might choose a problem-solving task; other times we might select a straightforward computation problem because we want to hear the different strategies students use to solve it. As a coach, it's up to you to help guide the selection of the task toward what you think will be beneficial for your team.

You and your team might select a task from a written assessment if you are curious why students struggled on a particular question. Or, you might choose a task for a particular content area your team is interested in, such as fractions or ratios. You might choose a task because you are planning a lesson together and want to anticipate possible student strategies for a specific problem. And sometimes, you might choose tasks before a new unit because your team is curious what informal methods students might use to grapple with concepts they haven't been introduced to.

STEP 3 Practicing the Interview

Before actually interviewing students, it can be helpful to practice our interviewing skills. This rehearsal allows us to notice what types of questions we are asking. Practicing also can spark a discussion about the different types of questions we may want to use and ones we might want to avoid.

STOP and JOT

What types of questions might you ask to uncover a student's thinking?
What types of questions might you avoid?

Here are some questions I have found helpful in eliciting students' thinking and some questions I try to avoid. You may want to add to the lists.

POSSIBLE QUESTIONS TO ASK

- What are you thinking?
- What do you predict will happen?
- Can you solve it in a different way?
- How do you know?
- How did you figure that out?
- Why did you . . . ? (write that, draw that, etc.)
- You wrote _____. Why? How did that help you?
- I noticed that you stopped what you were doing just now/crossed something out/erased. What were you thinking?
- Why did you change your mind/answer?
- I don't know what you mean by that. Can you explain?
- Can you use a picture to represent your thinking?
- Can you justify your work with the manipulatives in front of you?
- Are you sure of your answer? How do you know?
- What do you notice?
- Is there another way to justify your work? What is it?

QUESTIONS/THINGS TO AVOID SAYING

- That's right!
- Good job!
- What if you . . . ?
- You know that if you just . . .
- Remember what we did in class last week . . .
- And (what you've written) is just another way to say . . .
- Oh, I see what you did. You . . .
- Do you mean . . . ?

These lists are just meant to be guides and to provide some question stems to think about. You may want to ask your colleagues to participate in a brainstorming session similar to the previous Stop and Jot and to compile their own questions that uncover student thinking. As they brainstorm, you can pose additional questions from the previous list and ask whether or not they will elicit student thinking. You also may want to give an example of a leading question and then ask the group why we may want to avoid those. Afterward the team can brainstorm other questions they may want to avoid. Charting or recording the types of questions that can uncover student thinking as well as ones we think might not be as useful can be an ongoing reference for the team.

After a discussion of the different types of questions, I group teachers into threes. One teacher plays the student, another plays an interviewer, and the third is the observer, who records the questions asked throughout the interview. We practice the tasks we will use with students. We then switch roles so that each member has a chance to be the student, teacher, and observer. After we have rotated the roles, I pose questions to the teams to debrief.

FACILITATION QUESTIONS for the Interview Role-Play Debrief

?

? Look through the observers' recording. Note which questions were probing or leading. How might we change the leading questions?

? What was challenging about conducting the interview?

? Do we need to make any adjustments to the task?

I like this step of practicing the interviews and debriefing because it allows us to give one another feedback in small groups. However, I have also skipped this step on some occasions for time purposes. If you skip it, you may want to consider taking time after the first student interview to reflect on the previous questions as well as the debrief questions.

STEP 4 Selecting Students

Just as selecting a task is important, so is selecting the students. Which students you choose to interview depends on what your goals are. For example, if your goal is to figure out why students struggled with a particular task or test, it can be helpful to interview some students who got stuck as well as some students who answered correctly. This juxtaposition allows you to think about the contrast between the two responses. If your goal is to examine your students' prior knowledge about an upcoming topic, it can help to survey a range of students who might have different experiences.

Initially, it helps to choose students who are comfortable thinking aloud and who are more verbal. However, quieter students can and do open up when they are sitting one-on-one for interviews. In these cases, I sometimes don't have the whole team in the room if I think a student might be nervous. Instead, we can video the interview and then watch it as a team. We usually try to interview three students for 5–10 minutes each, which allows us to have a variety of students' thinking to examine.

STEP 5 Conducting the Interviews

Before the student comes in, it can be important to remind everyone that the goal of the interview is *not* to teach the student. This constraint is often hard for the team, but the end goal of the interview is learning how the student thinks, which will eventually improve their teaching. You also may want to remind teachers that it's important not to assume that the student is thinking the way the teachers think they are. Sometimes we see a student's action and assume a meaning, but it's important to check our assumptions by asking students why they are doing something. For example, we may see a student using fingers or counters and assume they are counting by ones, but they may be counting by fives.

It can be helpful to designate one person to start the interview and ask the initial questions. When you and the student are more comfortable, everyone can jump in, but initially, it can throw off the student's train of thought. I usually start by doing the first interview myself. You may want to practice several times and videotape yourself before doing it with the team, or you may want to do it all together and learn together.

Often, we set up a video camera before the student comes in. I really push for the use of video during the interview because it allows us to go back and listen to a student's response if we aren't sure we heard it correctly at first. The recording also allows us to review and examine our questions. Finally, recording an interview sets the stage for using video later on. This is a low-risk video situation, and as we move to asking teachers to video their teaching practice, this little step can be helpful in moving toward using video of our classrooms to discuss teaching and learning. If you aren't going to videotape the interview, make sure someone is designated to take really thorough notes.

When the student comes in, it helps to start off the interview by letting the student know what to expect. Students may or may not be used to being questioned about their thinking, so it's important to tell them that we want them to think out loud as they work. You also may want to tell students that when the team asks a question, it doesn't mean the student is wrong or right—you are just trying to figure out what is going on in their brains. You may want to give them a pen to work with, rather than a pencil, so they can't erase their thinking and we have a record of it. They can just make an X to cross out anything they want. (Some teachers have even started using pens in their math classrooms after we started using pens in these interviews.)

Once the student is settled and knows what to expect, they then read the problem aloud, or one of team members reads the problem to the student, depending on the comfort level of the student and their reading skills. The team watches the student solve the problem, listens to their thinking, and asks clarifying or probing questions as needed. It's really hard to resist praising or asking leading questions. Even after doing hundreds of these interviews, I still find myself sometimes accidentally encouraging a student down a certain path. It's also hard to balance giving students wait time and knowing when to probe the student to think aloud. Finally, it's important not to encourage students either verbally or nonverbally, because this can alter their thinking. Resist the desire to encourage or discourage certain answers and praise students.

What's interesting about the student interview is that it differs from observing a student or looking at student work. We are able to probe and ask questions so that we can really get inside how a student is solving a problem. Often, we find that the student knows more or less than the written work indicates. For example, a student might write a correct equation but not be able to explain the concept behind it. Similarly, a student might turn in blank papers with just an answer but actually use sophisticated mental math strategies that they aren't sure how to record.

After the interview is done, we always thank the student and then either bring in another student or start the debrief, depending on what time allows. Usually, the interviews take no more than ten minutes each.

What follows is an example of an interview that was conducted with a sixth-grade student. The team was planning a unit on negative and positive integers and wanted to know what students might know about the topic before any formal instruction. As you read it, think about how the team set the expectations for the interview, encouraged the student to explain their thinking, and asked clarifying and probing questions as the student worked. Also think about where the team might have missed opportunities to ask further questions, or how you might have conducted the interview differently.

Mr. B: We are all just curious to see where you are at and what your thinking is when you see a problem like this. Take a couple of minutes, think it over, and try to figure out a solution. Then you will talk us through what you were thinking and how you got it. And if you don't know something, feel free to say "I'm not sure about it." Can you start by reading the problem to us?

Student: Negative 3 plus 5.

Mr. B: You have a sheet of paper. Take some think time, think it over, then start working it out, and then you can let us know what you think the solution is and how you went about solving it.

Student: 2.

Mr. B: OK. Write down your solution and then walk us through how you did that or what you were thinking in your head. In other words, show your work.

Student starts writing −3, −2, −1 . . .

Student: Does zero count?

Mr. B: Do you think zero counts?

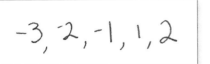

Figure 2.1 Student's solution to −3 + 5

Student doesn't say anything. Continues writing. 1, 2.

Mr. B: Could you walk us through what you were doing there? (points to numbers written down in Figure 2.1)

Student: Basically, because I know that if you were to subtract a negative number you go back, it would be greater, well, technically less, but if you add it, it would go from negative 3 to negative 2 to negative 1, then to 1 then to 2.

Ms. M: What about the zero? You had asked a question about the zero. What was going on in your head when you said, "Oh, does zero count?"

Student: Like, if zero counts as one of the numbers, you would add. So, the answer would be either be 2 or 1.

Ms. M: So, are you sure of your answer? Are you 100 percent sure it's 2?

Student: Umm . . . 90 percent.

Mr. B: If you put the zero into the problem, would your answer change?

Student: Yes. The answer would be 1.

Mr. B: We have one more problem. Can you start by reading it out loud to us?

Student: Negative 10 plus negative 2.

Mr. B: Take some time to think it over, come up with your solution, and walk us through your thinking again.

Student: I got negative 12.

Mr. B: Can you explain what you did?

Student: I know there is a negative sign, so I believe you would, um . . . you would add both negatives together, and it would become a less number. And then, so I just . . . I don't know how to say it.

Ms. M: Instead of saying it, can you show us?

Student writes their work, shown in Figure 2.2.

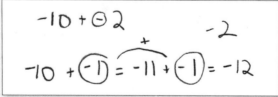

Figure 2.2 Student's solution to −10 + −2

Student: So, I know that negative 1 plus negative 1 would be negative 2.

Ms. M: Great. Thank you.

STOP and JOT

What do you notice about the interview? What did you notice about the student's strategies? How did the team set expectations for the student? What questions did they ask that uncovered student thinking? What missed opportunities were there to uncover more about the student's thinking?

You may have noticed that the team members set clear expectations for the student to explain their work. You may have also noticed that the team did not answer the student's question or attempt to teach them. In addition, they asked some questions that uncovered student thinking, such as "Can you explain what you did?" or "Can you show us?" However, you also may have thought of some additional questions the team could have asked after the student explained their solution to the second problem. For example, you may have wanted to know more about how the student used the −2 to help them think about the problem. You also may have wanted to know more about what the student meant when they said, "It would be greater, well, technically less." The team's interview skills will develop over time, and the process allows them to focus not only on the strategies the student is using but also on the types of questions they are asking, especially after the interview, in the debrief.

STEP 6 Analyzing the Interview

After the student leaves, we debrief what we noticed and determine what questions we have. Our goal is to analyze what the student was saying to figure out something about the student's thinking related to the mathematical concept. Often the first step is making sure that we all understood the way in which the student attempted to solve the problem. I find myself asking clarifying questions like, "What was the student doing when they wrote −3, −2, −1, 1, 2?" or "Why did the student talk about −1 plus −1?"

After we agree on the student's overall strategy, we move to inferring how the student might have been thinking. For example, in the debrief for the interview described earlier, I asked, "When the student wrote the numbers −3, −2, −1, 1, 2, I noticed he was struggling with what to do with the zero. Why do you think that was?" Someone said, "I think he was struggling because he didn't know how to count up when there were negative numbers and he needed to move to positive numbers. I wonder if a number line would help?"

My role as the coach is to facilitate the meeting, keep us focused on the mathematical thinking, and bring any research or conceptual ideas I might know to the table. For example, I might name certain strategies we see so that we all have a way to talk about what students are doing. Or I might note that the research confirms a hypothesis we have about students' difficulties with the tasks. In the previous example, I brought up the research related to difficulties students often have with ordering rational numbers and asked the teachers to look at some of the strengths and challenges the student demonstrated related to this. I also named "decomposition" and "counting up" as strategies and asked the team to think about how they helped the student think about the second problem.

The way I facilitate meetings is to ask questions. I try not to talk too much but instead create opportunities for the team to come to conclusions on their own. Some questions that may help you guide the debrief meetings follow.

FACILITATION QUESTIONS for Student Interview Debrief

- ❓ What did you notice about the student's thinking?
- ❓ What questions do you still have?
- ❓ What questions did the interviewer ask that seemed to uncover the student's thinking?
- ❓ What models did the student use to think with?
- ❓ What kind of reasoning did the student use?
- ❓ In what ways do the student's explanations make sense?
- ❓ What different conceptions do you notice the student has? What interventions might be helpful if we notice these ideas in our classrooms?

(continued)

❓ What implications does what we learned have for our work moving forward with students?

❓ What are some next steps for our learning?

In addition to talking about the mathematical content of the interview, it can be helpful to talk about our questioning. Often someone will say, "I wish we asked the student about . . ." In the earlier example, the team wanted to know more about what the student meant when they said "technically less." We discussed how difficult it can be to remember to ask these questions in the moment and made a note to remind us to ask students to explain what they mean when we don't understand something.

Finally, we talk about what implications these interviews have for our planning. In the previous example, the team interviewed three students. Each interview took approximately 5–10 minutes. It was interesting to see what their intuitions were before we introduced any models, and we then had a variety of solutions to discuss. For example, one student drew a number line to solve the problems, and we saw potential in that strategy. We decided to use our next planning meeting to explore different ways to use the number line in the upcoming unit.

During the meeting, you may want to take notes or record the discussion. That way after the meeting, you can share notes from the discussion as well as any next steps the team has decided on.

THE OUTCOME: SPARKING CURIOSITY

As a teacher, student interviews were a valuable tool for me because I learned to listen to my students and understand their thinking. Interviews have been equally useful for me as a coach because they solved a major challenge for me— how do I foster curiosity about student learning in the teacher team? It's so hard to be curious about student learning when you are under pressure from so many outside forces. However, interviews allowed us to separate from the classroom and wonder about how students were thinking.

The rise in curiosity didn't happen right away. As soon as we left the meeting, teachers went back to face the realities of the classroom. But the more students we interviewed, the more teams began to say things like, "We should interview some kids about this test question" or "I wonder if they would really solve the problem using a number line. Can we interview some kids and see what they would do with the number line for this task?" I heard less of "My kids can't do that" and more of "I don't think they will solve it that way, but let's bring some students in and ask." We were often surprised, myself included, by students' strategies, which further increased our curiosity.

These shifts were powerful for us as learners and also as teachers because they impacted the questions we asked our students in class. An administrator noted to me that they'd observed teachers were more likely to ask students, "How did you get that answer?" before trying to remediate or intervene. Student interviews, on their own, are certainly not going to completely change a school or teacher, but they are a step in the direction of learning together and focusing on student thinking. In the next tool, we will talk about how to maintain this focus on student thinking and collaborative learning as we visit classrooms.

REFLECTING on LEARNING

- Try an interview on your own, and audiorecord it. Go back and listen to the questions you asked, and note any that were leading. Also note any missed opportunities. Then summarize what you learned about the student's thinking.

- How might you begin this work in your school or district? Is there a particular content area or grade level that might be beneficial to start with?

- How will you know whether the work is successful?

EXPLORING the LITERATURE

The way student interviews are described in this chapter is similar in some ways to how *clinical interviews* are used by researchers. The term *clinical* is used because the interviews take place outside the natural setting of the classroom. Clinical interviews were originally used by Piaget: he found that listening to children think aloud helped him learn about student thinking and child development. Researchers still use them as a tool to create *explanatory models* of how students think about different mathematical ideas (Ginsburg 1997). Researchers have also studied their use as professional development tools.

Studies have found that the use of these types of interviews in professional development can help teachers develop a better understanding of how students think and learn about mathematics and problem-solving (Heng and Sudarshan 2013; Hunting 1997; Jacobs et al. 2007; McDonough et al. 2002). As teachers develop an understanding of student thinking through conducting and analyzing interviews, they move toward more interpretive listening in their classrooms, plan lessons that are focused on students' needs, and develop awareness that they can build upon students' informal ideas and connect them to formal content. You may want to read some of these research articles to see how others have used interviews in their coaching and professional development. I also wrote a short article titled "Learn to Listen" in The Learning Professional (2020) that you may find helpful.

If you are looking to lead a book study with a team, I have found the Cognitively Guided Instruction books helpful, in particular Carpenter et al.'s *Children's Mathematics: Cognitively Guided Instruction* (2014). In addition, Marilyn Burns and Lynn Zolli have created a digital interview tool called *Listening to Learn* (2021), which includes videos that can be useful for teams to watch before conducting their own interviews.

VISITING CLASSROOMS
Developing Your Lens

enter Ms. Mac's fifth-grade classroom and immediately sit down on the rug with a small group of students who are looking at a picture of a large basket of apples. Underneath the basket are twelve smaller baskets with different students' names on each one.

"I notice all of our names are on the baskets!" Evelyn says.

"I wonder whether each person is going to get the same amount of apples from the big basket." Joe adds.

"I wonder if Ms. Mac is going to tell us how many apples are in that big basket." Rory notes.

As I sit with the group, I take notes of what students are saying and snap pictures of their notebooks (Figure 3.1).

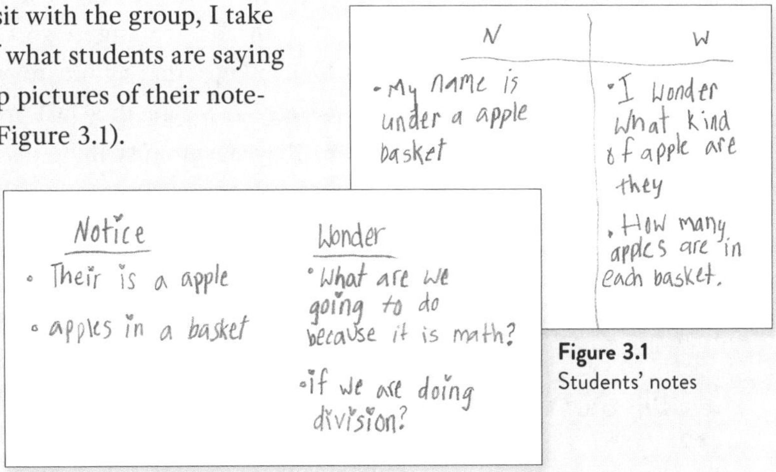

Figure 3.1
Students' notes

Ms. Mac circulates and listens in to students' thinking, asking clarifying and probing questions to the groups. She then brings the groups back together and asks students to share their responses with the whole class. After a few shares, she asks Jayvon to share what he told his group. He answers, "I told them I wondered how many apples each of us are going to get." Many of the students use hand signals to show they agree with Jayvon.

After some more discussion, Ms. Mac tells the students that there are 204 apples in the big basket. Students head back to their tables to investigate Jayvon's question, which Ms. Mac wrote on the board: "How many apples will each student get in their basket?" Base-ten blocks, coffee filters, chart paper, and markers are available on students' tables.

I move to sit with a different group and ask, "Can you explain to me what you are working on?"

"Sure. Ms. Mac went apple picking this weekend and picked 204 apples. We are trying to figure out how many apples we would each get if she split them up equally into these baskets," Maria tells me.

The students go back to working, and I record their discussions.

Justin says to the group, "I'm not good at division, and I think this is a division problem."

Maria responds, "So use the blocks or draw a picture."

Justin then sets out twelve coffee filters for the twelve baskets and places one ten-stick in each basket, as seen in Figure 3.2. He then tries to place another ten-stick in each. "I ran out of ten-sticks—that's not going to work. Do I have to break them all up? That's going to take *forever*."

Tom suggests maybe they just pretend each cube is a five. They start to distribute the fives and are having a bit of trouble keeping track. Maria volunteers to record the total as they go on.

As I leave the classroom, I can't wait to talk to the grade team about how the students were making sense of the problem and the different strategies they were using to solve the problem. I also jot down some notes about number choice. I wonder whether these numbers were the best choice for the task. I also

Figure 3.2
Students working with manipulatives

wonder how we could help students make connections between the base-ten blocks strategy and the algorithm some of them used. I make a note to share with the team some ideas about different strategies for orchestrating a discussion.

HOW CAN WE DEVELOP OUR COACHING SKILLS THROUGH CLASSROOM VISITS?

Visiting classrooms like Ms. Mac's is the best part of my job as a coach. Without the pressure of teaching or managing a classroom of students, I can watch, talk, and listen to students. In each of these visits, an opportunity exists for me to learn something new about how students think. However, when I first started visiting classrooms as a new coach, I missed many of these chances because I wasn't focusing my attention on the students. Instead, I was looking closely at teacher moves. I was finding evidence of specific practices so that I could give detailed feedback to the teacher. I noticed what questions they asked, what techniques they used to engage the class, and what routines and systems they put in place. These observations had value, but a big change in both my coaching and learning occurred when I shifted my focus from what the teachers were doing to what the students were doing.

When I made this shift, I learned more about how students think about problems, about how certain tasks allow for different types of thinking, and about all the intuitive strategies students bring to problems before they are introduced to formal methods of solving them. I was reminded that students are capable of far more than I ever thought they were. I also learned that I really needed to *listen to students* and not *listen for answers*, which we discussed in Tool 2: Student Interviews. Shifting attention to the student changes the type of learning that occurs in classroom visits as well as in interviews.

This shift also improved the feedback I gave teachers. What I noticed about student learning was connected to what the teacher was doing, or not doing, and our conversations and debriefs changed to focus on these noticings. The next steps about what the teacher could do to support learning grew out of our discussions, so they were grounded in what would best support the students in the classroom, based on their mathematical thinking. This readjustment also took the focus off the teacher and the teaching and put it on the students and the learning.

In addition to the collaborative learning the teacher and I enjoying during these debriefs, I learning a lot about how kids thought about math. I understood new strategies for solving problems, and I saw approaches I hadn't anticipated. My learning was so powerful that I wanted to share with teachers. It bothered me that I learned so much from visiting their classrooms mostly because I could just listen to the students and ignore all the aspects of running a classroom. I thought about how I could share these learning opportunities with teachers as part of my coaching. In Tool 4 I'll share more about how I use learning walks to bring teams of teachers into classrooms to give them these learning opportunities as well. However, before we talk about facilitating learning walks with a team of teachers, I want to talk about how I developed my skills as an observer and listener, and how I used that learning to improve my coaching and, ultimately, my teachers' pedagogy.

STOP and JOT

 Think about the opening vignette—the apples lesson. What do you notice about the description of the classroom? How is it different from visits where the focus is on giving feedback to the teacher?

The main thing that stands out to me is the difference in perspective. Imagine your coaching lens as a camera lens. Often, when we visit classrooms, we zoom in our lens on the teacher, and the students are blurry in the background. In the previous scenario, I used my lens to focus on the students, with the teacher in the background. She's still in the picture, but she's not the focus of it. She is the one who created the task and chose the manipulatives on the table. She selected the students who shared their wonderings. However, the students and their thinking were my focus. Zooming in on students allows us to think deeply about what they are doing and then pushes us to think about how teachers can support students' thinking. It puts the learning first and then allows us to look at the teaching to determine how it is fostering, or how it can better foster, the learning.

In addition, when I zoom in on students, I think about how to support learning across classrooms instead of just thinking about how I can support one individual teacher. After this visit, I can visit the rest of the grade-level team and see how students are making sense of division problems in those classes. Later, I can analyze how students are making sense of division problems as a grade and think about the implications for planning and instruction. Did the Notice and Wonder help students make sense of the problem more than the act-it-out strategy down the hall? Why? Why not? What can we learn from the students in one another's classes? These visits can build your knowledge of different student strategies and help you think about how to best support your teams.

CLASSROOM VISITS IN ACTION

Whenever I start work with a new school or team, it is helpful for me to visit as many classrooms as I can. If possible, I try to visit after I have done some of the relationship-building work that I described in Tool 1, which allows teachers to feel more comfortable with my presence in the room. When I start a series of visits in a school, I use the following five steps to guide my work:

STEP 1 Communicate with the team

STEP 2 Determine a focus for visits

STEP 3 Collect data

STEP 4 Analyze data

STEP 5 Summarize and share

As you read through the specifics of each of these steps, you may find the Visiting Classrooms Planning Template to be helpful. You can find it in Appendix 3 and on the 6 Tools website. I like to use it to sketch out my plan for the visits before I begin. Writing out a learning plan allows me to be clear on my goals and plan at the start of the work. You may find it helpful to jot ideas down on it as you read through the different steps.

STEP 1 Communicate with the Team

When I first start working with a school or district, I visit classrooms to build relationships, observe the culture of the school, and learn about the classrooms and children in the building. Before I begin these visits, I try to be transparent with teachers about why I want to visit their classrooms. I explain that I am learning new things. I am trying to create a culture of learning within the school, and one way to do that is to model that I am always learning, practicing new skills, and sharing what I learn. I explicitly tell teachers that I'll be looking at students' thinking; I am not there to observe teachers or evaluate their teaching moves. It can be helpful to communicate the purpose of these visits in a department meeting or in an email.

I also introduce myself to students if I am new to the class or school when I come in for a visit. I usually say some version of this: "Good morning, Class 101. I'm Nicora, and I'm really interested in how people think about math, so I may ask you some questions about the problems you are working on. I hope you will share your thoughts with me." Sometimes the teachers do this introduction for me instead.

In addition to communicating with teachers and students, it's also important for me to collaborate with the administrative team in the building. This team could involve the principal, assistant principal, and/or the instructional cabinet. I discuss the process with them and ask what they suggest I look for when I visit. For example, if they have invested a lot of time on incorporating small-group mathematical discussions into their lessons, I will look for that as I visit. Often, the administrators want to accompany me, but I encourage them to allow me to visit classrooms on my own and collect data before I talk with them about their impressions of the learning in the school. Otherwise, I find I can be swayed by their statements. For example, they might tell me that Ms. H is their best math teacher, and then I find I subconsciously look for data to confirm that view.

After my visit, it is important to norm my noticings and feedback with the admin team to ensure that we are all on the same page about what we see when we visit a classroom, but initially I want to get a picture of the school on my own. Visiting alone also helps me develop a coach–teacher relationship and differentiate coaching visits from evaluative administrative visits. Teachers have a range of experiences (good and bad) with visits from administrators, and possibly with other coaches, that may be similar or different from your visits. Doing the visits solo allows you to create the norms surrounding your coaching visits.

STEP 2 Determine a Focus for Visits

When planning your visits, it can be helpful to think of a question you want to answer by visiting these classrooms. For the first round of visits, I find that using a general guiding question enables me to collect data about the school and allows for interesting patterns to emerge. Here are some sample questions that I've used when visiting a school for the first time:

- What are students learning about what it means to do mathematics?
- What are students learning about the particular mathematical concept they are working on during my visit?
- How are students making sense of problems?
- How are students discussing and talking about mathematics with one another?

STOP and JOT

 What are some other questions you might use as you visit the classrooms? How might you modify the previous questions to meet the needs of your teams?

STEP 3 Collect Data

Once you have selected a question to focus on, you can think about what data you might collect to answer that question. *Data* is often so narrowly defined in our schools—we often mean test scores or student work from performance tasks. This information is one type of data, but it isn't the only kind. When I talk about collecting data during classroom visits, I'm thinking of the wide range of information a researcher might collect, which could be qualitative or quantitative. Data could be a quote from a student or a puzzled look you noticed on a student's face. It could be the way the students first arranged fraction tiles or the way the students organized the problem on their paper. It could be any information that helps you understand what students are *thinking*. You can't always determine their thoughts from a list of answers. You may need to ask students to show

73

their work or explain how they arrived at their answer. Sometimes I need to ask clarifying questions so that I can understand how they are thinking. I also try to operate under the principle that students do what makes sense to them (even if it causes them to arrive at the wrong answer), so I keep asking questions until I can understand their process. You also may want to take photos of their work because sometimes it's difficult to figure out why they solved a problem a certain way, and you may want to think about it more later or to ask someone else about it.

I've found the Standards for Mathematical Practices (SMP) helpful in thinking about what data to collect during visits. For example, I might focus on SMP 1 ("Make sense of problems and persevere in solving them") and collect observations of students making sense of problems. What indicators would provide evidence of sense-making? For example, if students are making sense of problems, we would expect to see them

- finding entry points into the problem.
- making conjectures about a problem.
- analyzing information in the problem.
- explaining the task in their own words.

Naming indicators before the visit helps me be clear on what I am listening and looking for and can help guide questions I might ask students. In this case, I might ask students to explain the task in their own words, so I can record what they say. Their answers are my data. Sometimes I share the indicators with teachers so that they are reminded that I am looking at student work and not evaluating their teaching. Other times, I chose not to share them if I am concerned that teachers will alter their instruction to address the indicators. I suggest you think about your relationships with the team members and their experiences with classroom visits when deciding what to share with them.

To keep myself organized, I use a low-inference observation template for taking notes. I want evidence of student thinking, so I record what they say, what they do, and what tasks they are working on. These notes plus photographs of their work will especially help you look back and reflect later if, like me, you don't have the best memory! Including time stamps in your notes also allows you to track how much time students are spending on various tasks.

Table 3.1 shows an example from one of my visits to a third-grade classroom. My actual notes from the visit were taken with paper and pencil and weren't written in complete sentences, but for clarity purposes, I cleaned them up. Also, my handwriting is terrible, so I often type up my notes after a visit if I am sharing them with a teacher so that they can easily read what I wrote. I know that many people use computers when visiting classrooms to eliminate this step, but I find it can be intimidating for teachers when I take my laptop out and start taking notes when I first visit a classroom. The laptop also limits where I can sit, and it doesn't allow me to move around the room easily, so I usually choose not to use one. Whatever method you use to take notes, make sure you move around and sit with students, which further distinguishes your visit from the type of visit an administrator would do. It can be hard to transcribe everything in the moment, but get down as much as you can. With practice, you will develop shorthand tricks that make sense to you. Immediately after leaving the room, you can clean up what you've written while it's still fresh in your mind.

Table 3.1 Sample notes from a classroom visit

CLASSROOM VISITED: 102	
Time	**Low-Inference Observations**
10:00	Students were shown an image of two number lines and asked to turn and talk. The teacher, Ms. Zoe, said: "Let's take a look at these pictures. There are some things that are the same and some things that are different. With your turn-and-talk partner, talk about: What's the same about these number lines? What is different? I want to know what you think." Students started talking immediately. Turn and Talk: What's the same about these number lines? What's different? **Evie:** One has jumps that are big (used her hands to show) and one has jumps that are smaller. **Solomon:** Yeah, and the number lines are labeled different. One is labeled by 6s.

(continued)

Evie: They are both counting by 6.

Solomon: Yeah, but this one has 2 and 4 labeled, too.

10:05   Ms. Zoe clapped, and the students came back together.

Ms. Zoe: Ayla, can you tell me what you and your partner talked about?

Ayla: The one on the bottom is counting by 6 and so is the one on the top, but the one on the top goes by smaller numbers. It goes, 2, 4, 6, and the other goes 6, 12, 18.

Ms. Zoe: Yes. They have different *intervals*. This one is going by 6s but this one is going by 2s or 1s. Anyone notice anything different?

Martin: The second one goes to a bigger number.

Ms. Zoe: Yes. The first one goes to 24, and the second goes to 54. So, I have another question: which number line would be better for larger numbers?

Camille: The bottom one. The smaller the spaces, the more we can fit on the line.

Students use hand signals to show they agreed.

10:10   **Ms. Zoe:** That's a nice way to put it. These two are also showing us different equations. Which equation are they showing us?

Andy: The top one is 6 x 4.

Akim: No, it's 4 x 6. It's 4 jumps of 6. Can I come up and show you? The first number is how many jumps there are. 1, 2, 3, 4 (points to four jumps).

Ms. Zoe: OK. What about the 6?

Akim: You go up 6 in each and you get 24.

Ms. Zoe: Thanks for explaining that. Does everyone understand?

Most students nod or use hand signals to show they agree, but there are three girls in the back who have been quiet through most of the lesson.

STOP and JOT

🖉 Take a minute and jot down what you noticed about what I recorded.

What stands out most to me about low-inference notes is that they are specific, objective descriptions of what is occurring in the room without an evaluative opinion of what is occurring. The low-inference observations are not a time for you to say the task was boring or exciting or the teacher was amazing or ineffective. They should be just a description of what is happening. It can be hard not to write evaluative comments. I had to retrain myself after I spent a lot of time doing individual coaching visits. I was so focused on looking for "glows and grows" in those visits that it was hard for me to step out of that role and switch to gathering information about the students. Over time, it has gotten easier to recognize the difference.

For example, here are some additional examples of low-inference observations, as well as observations that are not low-inferences:

- A pair of students was using a number line to add 5 + 9 by placing their finger on the five and making nine hops until they landed on 14.
- Students were asked to turn and talk to a partner about how Nicole and John's solutions were similar and different. Students said:
  - "I noticed Nicole used a table and John used a chart."
  - "I disagree with what Nicole did because I got a different answer."
- The teacher's questioning was highly effective.
- Students were bored.

STOP and JOT

What makes the first two observations low-inference? How could you change the third and fourth example so that they are less judgmental and more low inference?

You may have noticed that the first two observations included specific strategies and student quotes without any evaluative statements. On the other hand, the last two comments did not include specific details and provided judgment statements (positive and negative) about the teacher or students. Our goal when taking notes is to record data that is specific and nonjudgmental so that we can analyze what is going on objectively.

In addition to recording your observations, you may want to ask students about what they are doing if you need further evidence. You don't want to ask leading questions, but you may want to ask what they are working on or ask clarifying questions about their mathematical thinking. Some examples of how to probe students' thinking include:

- Tell me about this problem you are working on.
- What are you and your partner talking about?
- What has the class been working on in math today?
- Why did you add those numbers?
- How do you know that works?

The answers to these questions may provide you with some additional insight into students' thinking that will help you make sense of what is going on in the classroom.

STEP 4 Analyze Data

Analyzing the data occurs on two levels. First, you can synthesize your notes from the individual classroom visits. Then, after you have completed multiple visits, you can analyze the data across the different classrooms you visit. These two steps can make the process more organized and can help you keep track of your thoughts.

Analyze Individual Classroom Data

Immediately after leaving the classroom, as part of cleaning up my observation notes and student responses, I write at least one summary statement about what I noticed that can help answer the guiding question. I like to start these statements with "Students were . . ." This frame helps keep my focus on what the students were doing and saying.

STOP and JOT

 Look through the notes from the lesson in Table 3.1. What might be one summary statement you might make after leaving the classroom?

These are some summary statements I wrote after the lesson:

- Students were able to notice multiple similarities and differences between the two number lines and determine which might be better for larger numbers. All pairs were able to get started on this task and name at least one similarity or difference.

- Students were able to connect the representation to a multiplication expression and connect the representation to groups and numbers in a group.

- Most students participated throughout the lesson, but three girls did not participate and were not called on or addressed by the teacher.

After recording some summary statements, you may also want to write any questions or wonderings you have. I try to make these questions more general, so they are relevant to more than just this lesson. As I look through my notes, I think about what opportunities exist for us to learn more about a particular math content area, or about student thinking, or about representations that make thinking visible.

STOP and JOT

 What are some questions or wonderings you have after reading the notes in Table 3.1? What learning opportunities do you see?

Here are some questions I wondered about from the previous lesson:

- How can we help students formalize their thinking using precise mathematical language (such as *interval*)?

- How might we connect this representation to other representations students are using for multiplication?

- How might we use this opportunity to talk about the commutative property?

- How can we think about participation and related equity questions together? Who speaks? Who listens? Whose voices are amplified?

The summary statements and questions might help you focus on big ideas that you think the entire team can learn from or investigate. Consolidating your notes immediately after classroom visits allows you to have a brief summary of each visit that you can refer to when analyzing trends across classrooms, so you don't have to look back through all of the individual notes.

Analyze Across Classrooms

After you have visited all the classrooms, it's time to analyze the data you have collected. Look through and write out all of your summary statements and questions from your visits on chart paper or your computer. Organizing them by grades or grade bands can be helpful. Then you can start to search for patterns and brainstorm next steps.

Let's say the question I was focusing on was "How do students at this school make sense of and solve problems?" I'll draw on the indicators and subquestions I generated before the classroom visits to help me find patterns. For example, I might look closely at the following:

- How often were students given opportunities to solve problems?

- How challenging were these problems?

- What types of tools were they using to help solve the problems?

- What types of strategies did they use?

- How successful were they at solving problems?

- What challenges did they face in solving them?

- Who participated during the lesson? What opportunities were there for students to explain their ideas or comment on other's ideas?

- Did all students have equal access to the lesson and discussion? Could everyone get started on the task?

- Did all students get to engage in the cognitive challenge of the task or was it overscaffolded for some?
- Were any students' voices privileged during the discussion? Were any ignored?
- How were students recognized as being able to contribute to the discussion?

The main goals here are (1) to use evidence to support any claims you make and (2) to think about the type of learning the team might want to engage in based on what you noticed. For example, you might notice patterns developing about tasks. Perhaps students in the lower grades struggled with tasks at first but were given tools, such as number lines, to help them when they were struggling. You might also notice that students in the upper grades also struggled with tasks but were not given tools and became frustrated. This evidence might lead you to think about how you could build on the lower grade's use of supports for the upper grades.

STEP 5 Summarize and Share

After each round of visits, you'll learn something new about what it means to do math in the school or district or about how students reason and think about different mathematical content. It can be helpful to record what you learned and cite specific examples of what you saw. Sometimes I share these notes directly with the admin team, sometimes I keep these notes for myself, and other times I share them with the teacher teams. The decision of whom to share with will be based on your relationships with the team members, their relationships with each other, and the culture of the school or district. No matter how I share them, I always use the summaries to plan next steps for the team and for individual teachers.

Let's look at an example of visits I recently did with a new coach and see how we planned and prioritized work from there.

THE OUTCOME: THE STORY OF KATHY

Kathy was a brand-new instructional coach in a K–8 school. Prior to taking on this role, she worked in the school as a kindergarten and second-grade teacher. She has served as a teacher at the school since it opened and has strong relationships with most teachers in the building and with the four administrators. The building has never had a full-time instructional coach but has had outside part-time literacy and math coaches over the years. Previously, I worked with the school as a math coach on a weekly basis, and now I provide support for Kathy's development as a coach.

When she first took on her new role, I suggested Kathy build her observation skills by visiting every classroom in the building during math and collecting evidence about what it meant to do mathematics at the school. We originally planned to have this step completed by the end of the first month of school, but that proved to be unrealistic. Immediate needs of teachers came first. Kathy also was tasked with mentoring teachers who needed support setting up structures and routines, helping teachers with a new reading program, and organizing and distributing a closet full of math manipulatives. She was also trying to build relationships with teachers and navigate the tensions that exist as she tried to meet the needs of both the administrators and the teachers in the school. She scheduled classroom visits between these other tasks and completed the visits toward the end of the second month of school. I accompanied her on some of these visits so that we could discuss and compare what we noticed.

Kathy sat with the kids during visits, recorded her low-inference notes in her notebook, and summarized the visits afterward. In addition to taking low-inference notes about the students, she identified one thing each teacher was especially strong at. She created this list so that she could later use it to identify which teachers might be able to assist with leading PD on particular topics and so she could recommend classrooms for intervisitation sites. For example, when Ms. M used Number Talks at the start of a lesson, students were able to explain their thinking in different ways. Therefore, if teachers had questions about building fluency or number sense, Kathy could suggest they visit Ms. M.

After all the visits, we met to discuss her findings and to create next steps. We looked at the findings holistically and decided to create next steps for grade bands (K–2, 3–5, 6–8) and then next steps for individual teachers as needed. Although we noticed the needs for the grade bands were very different, we tied all our next steps to the school's instructional focus and vision, which was to create a community of problem-solvers.

For our purposes, let's look at just the K–2 band. One thing Kathy noticed from the teachers in the K–2 classrooms was that in many classrooms, students did not have opportunities to participate because the conversations were very teacher-directed. One strategy was modeled, and then students practiced it. Students weren't allowed time to explore problems, and multiple strategies were not encouraged. Her evidence of this observation included comments made by the students when asked how they got their answer, such as, "This is the way you have to do it," or "We always have to put the answer after the equals sign."

In one classroom, students read a word problem and then were told to chant "*How many* means to subtract" before solving the problem. However, in another classroom, students were engaged in center time, where they explored many different ways to use blocks to make a certain number. Later, they were asked to convince the class why their answer was correct, which they did.

Kathy and I talked about the inequity of the experiences that students were getting in these different classrooms, and then we brainstormed possible solutions. We decided that instead of beginning with individual coaching, we would do a lesson study to leverage the group's knowledge. We wanted the team to hear how others plan and implement a lesson and to see what it looks like when students are given opportunities to explore and investigate mathematics without explicit teacher direction or modeling of a strategy. Therefore, we decided to focus the lesson study on ways to support young students to reason mathematically. We strategically planned in which classroom the lesson would be conducted (one of the classrooms where students were not given many opportunities to make sense). Our goal was that the whole-group planning and implementation of the lesson would help us learn from one another. We also decided that we would teach the lesson and make ourselves vulnerable to trying out new routines with the students in case they didn't work.

Anyone who has ever worked with me knows I am terrified of teaching very young students! I will teach a middle school class any day, but give me first graders and I panic. We knew that the teachers knew this about me, and we thought it would help us reinforce a culture of risk-taking because it would show how I am willing to do something outside of my comfort zone to learn something new. It also takes away the notion that this is a "model lesson" and instead gives them a chance to really focus on what students are thinking and saying during the lesson.

Our next step would be to follow up with visits to see the impact of the lesson study and then provide individual coaching support and feedback as needed. This process of starting with a whole-grade-band activity and then providing individual coaching support is similar to how I teach: let's start with the whole-class conversation and see what we learn from one another, then let's try it out and practice, and if we need individual support after we try it out individually, we can figure out what the individual interventions are.

The needs of the 3–5 and 6–8 grade bands were very different, but we followed a similar process. We looked at the observation notes, made summary statements, and then planned next steps for the team and for individual teachers. We then presented our ideas to the administrators so they could support our work and give us feedback about the impact of the lesson studies and coaching. The involvement of the administration team in the process will vary from school to school.

Kathy found that conducting the visits in this way created strong relationships with the teachers. They were open to having her visit their classrooms, and her role as a coach (as opposed to an evaluator) was made evident. In addition, this process gave her a focus for her coaching work. She had specific goals for the different grade band teams that were based on evidence she collected. These goals made her coaching purposeful, helped her choose activities to support teacher learning, and also allowed her to think about where she might need to develop her own skills by researching different ideas to bring to the team. Finally, she learned a lot about the various ways students think about math problems and increased her own understanding of students' mathematical strategies. It was particularly helpful for her to develop this knowledge about students in grade levels she had never taught herself.

My work with Kathy is one example of how classroom visits can be used strategically to develop relationships with teachers, learn about student thinking, and start planning overall next steps for a school. I know many of us want to get started right away with giving feedback and coteaching lessons—what we think is the "real work of coaching." However, taking time at the start of the year to be an observer and learner will pay off more substantially and intentionally for your overall coaching plan. In addition, these visits will become the basis for taking teams on learning walks so that they can have similar opportunities to learn from visiting classrooms. We'll talk more about that in Tool 4: Learning Walks.

REFLECTING on LEARNING

- What challenges might you face in creating summary statements? Go back to the low-inference observation in Table 3.1 and see if you can create an additional summary statement.

- Think about a recent classroom visit you had. How was it similar to the visits described here? How was it different?

- How might you incorporate these types of visits with more specific one-on-one coaching visits?

EXPLORING the LITERATURE

When talking to your administrator about your work, the research presented here may help you strengthen your case for spending time visiting classrooms to develop your noticing skills, and then later developing your teachers' skills. Research has shown that an important part of teaching is "noticing," or paying attention to what students say and do in the classroom (Erickson 2011; Sherin and Jacobs 2011; Santagata and Yeh 2016; Stahnke et al. 2016), including "sizing up students' ideas and responding" (Ball et al. 2001, 453). Mathematics teachers' ability to notice and be mindful of student thinking can be related to the quality of mathematics instruction (Mason 2002; Schoenfeld 2011).

Research also backs up my anecdotal evidence presented earlier that it's difficult for teachers to attend to, interpret, and respond to student thinking in the moment (Barnhart and van Es 2015; Jacobs and Empson 2016; Kang and Anderson 2015). Even experienced teachers find it difficult to comprehend students' strategies and hypothesize what students understand and don't understand as they are teaching.

Visiting classrooms and debriefing after gives us an opportunity to observe, reflect on, and analyze student thinking in a way that is very difficult to do while teaching. However, simply visiting classrooms and observing isn't enough. Sherin and van Es have done a lot of work exploring how teachers learn to notice different aspects of classroom interactions (Sherin and van Es 2005; van Es and Sherin 2010, 2021). They found a change in what teachers noticed after they participated in professional development in which they videotaped, watched, and discussed their practice. One of these shifts was that teachers moved from focusing on other teachers' actions to focusing on student thinking. In addition, at the start, teachers were reporting events. After professional learning, they moved to synthesizing and generalizing the events. A third shift was that teachers moved from giving evaluative comments to making comments based on evidence. These changes in what teachers noticed and how they analyzed these observations had a direct positive impact on their classroom practice.

Although this research focuses on teachers, we also need opportunities to further develop our noticing skills as coaches. These studies support the ideas in this section about the importance of you as a coach taking time to visit classrooms and watch students as they engage in mathematics. Developing your lens will also allow you to facilitate visits with teachers and help them develop their abilities to observe and analyze student thinking.

LEARNING WALKS
Focusing the Team on Students' Thinking

Tell me more about what we noticed about student engagement. Can we make any summary statements based on the evidence?" Ms. James, the building math coach, asks the team. Earlier in the day, they had visited three math classrooms together. During the visit, they took notes about what students were doing and saying. At the beginning of the debrief, teachers jotted statements from their observations on sticky notes. Now the team is standing together, looking for patterns in their collected notes.

"Class 601 had the most student engagement," Ms. C, a sixth-grade math teacher in her ninth year, says.

"Tell me more. What do you mean by 'engagement?' What were students doing and saying?" Ms. James responds.

"Well, on one of the sticky notes someone wrote that during independent think time, five of the six students at Table 1 were actively working on the problem. Three had used a table to solve, and two had used a graph. One of the students turned to his partner and said, 'I think I got it. Are you ready to discuss?' I think that shows engagement." Mr. M, a new teacher, responds.

"I think students were most engaged in that classroom because the task allowed almost everyone to start on the task. It had different ways to be solved, and so students who couldn't set up a proportion could make a table, or I even saw one student draw a picture. There were only two students in the whole class who weren't actively trying to solve the problem," Mr. L, a veteran teacher, notes.

"I agree! When we were in class 602, students were really bored. They were working on twenty problems where they had to solve for the missing value in the proportion. One student even said to me, 'I hate this class. It's so boring.' The worksheet didn't allow for different solution paths. It was very different from the task in class 601. But on the other hand, I do the same thing sometimes. Students need to practice skills," Ms. C says.

"Interesting point. So maybe we can think about that when we think about next steps. For now, let's record the summary statements about student engagement, and then we can focus on next steps. Remember, try to start them with 'Students were . . . ,'" Ms. James says.

The team then started to chart out some summary statements and next steps on the chart labeled "Student Engagement."

Ms. James and I debriefed her coaching after the visit. She said, "I think the visiting teachers learned more from the visit than the teacher who we visited did. We had a rich conversation about tasks and how to open them up." She paused. "It's interesting. We've had multiple PDs about opening up tasks and creating multiple entry points, but it wasn't really sticking for some teachers. I feel like seeing examples during the visits was really important in getting them to think about tasks."

Ms. James's feedback is similar to my experience doing learning walks with teams. I often hear from teachers how much they appreciate the opportunity to step back and watch and listen to students. Teams also enjoy discussing the visit with one another after they leave. Just like students need to discover and explore mathematics on their own, teachers need to learn about teaching through their experiences. And similar to how a teacher designs tasks that create opportunities for learning new mathematics, we, as coaches, can design and create opportunities for teacher teams to learn new ideas about teaching and learning. Learning walks are one way to create these opportunities.

HOW CAN WE DEVELOP OUR COACHING SKILLS THROUGH LEARNING WALKS?

Structured classroom visits with groups of teachers or administrators are often called *instructional rounds* or *learning walks*. The terms have somewhat different goals and processes. The types of collaborative visits I describe in this section are heavily informed by both these models but don't stay entirely true to either. I refer to them as "learning walks" because I like that the name focuses on *learning*. My goal is to focus collaborative visits on both student learning and the team's learning.

Lots of great resources are out there on instructional rounds and learning walks. If you have to choose two, I recommend *Instructional Rounds in Education: A Network Approach to Improving Teaching and Learning* by Elizabeth A. City, Richard F. Elmore, Sarah E. Fiarman, and Lee Teitel (2009) and *Teacher Rounds: A Guide to Collaborative Learning in and from Practice* by Thomas Del Prete (2013). Both books talk about instructional rounds at both the district level and the school level and give specific and practical suggestions. Of all the resources I have read, these guide my coaching work the most.

Instructional rounds are adapted from the medical rounds that take place in teaching hospitals. In medical rounds, a team visits patients, reviews the cases, asks questions, and discusses diagnosis and treatment. Similarly, instructional rounds involve teams visiting classrooms, collecting and analyzing data, and collaborating on next steps. The basic structure of an instructional round includes the following phases (City et al. 2009):

- Identify a problem of practice.
- Observe the current practice.
- Debrief the observation (this includes describing, analyzing, and predicting).
- Identify the next level of work.

When I do learning walks, I loosely follow these four steps, but I've adapted them so that they help us focus on learning and teaching math. Before I share, you may want to think about your own experiences with learning walks as well as what further modifications to the steps listed here that you might make for your own work.

STOP and JOT

What experiences have you had with learning walks? How are they similar to or different from these steps? How might you use or modify these steps for your context?

For me, the aspect of instructional rounds that resonated the most was how City and her colleagues framed the observations: "The single biggest observational discipline we have to teach people . . . is to look on top of the students' desks rather than the teacher at the front of the room" (2009, 30). Shifting the focus from what the *teacher* is doing to what the *students* are doing has been key for me in fostering learning among a team when we visit classrooms. It can be a big shift to move from examining *teaching* to focusing on *learning*. As we discussed in Tool 3: Visiting Classrooms, teachers, coaches, and administrators often focus on teacher moves when they visit classrooms. For example, a teacher might do an intervisitation and be asked to look at the questions the classroom teacher asked, the routines that are in place, or how the teacher introduced the lesson. These teacher-focused visits can be valuable, particularly for new teachers. However, visits that focus on students can complement teacher-focused visits and facilitate a different type of learning. When the lens shifts to foregrounding how students are answering questions, how they work through problems, or what discussions they are engaged in, the type of teacher learning that occurs differs. Looking at what students are saying and doing ultimately gives us information about teacher moves or strategies, but the path to thinking about these moves is different. Learning walks can help a team begin to shift toward looking at student thinking.

Learning walks also allow for a collaborative learning experience. Often-times, classroom visits appear to benefit only the person who is being observed.

In this model, the team doing the observing often learns more in their work together than the individual being observed.

Now that we have an idea of what a learning walk is and what the goals are, let's think about our role during the process.

The Role of the Coach

As a coach, you have the role of strategically planning and facilitating the learning walk. Using your knowledge of and goals for the team, you can plan the learning walk so the learning will be focused and relevant.

STOP and JOT

 Think about the initial vignette. What did you notice about Ms. James's role? What types of questions did she ask? How did she foster learning among the team?

What stands out to me in the vignette is that Ms. James played a similar role to that of a teacher in a math classroom. She was a facilitator of the learning. She guided the conversation by asking questions and pushing teachers to be specific, but she also allowed teachers to generate answers on their own. Not directly telling teachers what you want them to see can be frustrating because, as a coach, you want to push the team to certain conclusions. However, for learning walks to be successful, they need to be collaborative, and the teachers need opportunities to construct their own understanding. Like Ms. James, although I might strategically point out a few things I noticed or observed in the classroom, I try to focus on questioning and allow authentic discussion to take place so that learning can build from where teachers are and what they already know. I also jot down my own noticings and ideas and choose a few key points to bring up to the group.

More specifically, during the learning walk, it is important to

- assess what the team's current vision of teaching and learning is.
- help set the initial problem of practice or instructional focus using the school's vision and mission as a guide.
- provide activities and opportunities to norm what we listen and look for *before* we visit the classrooms.
- actively participate in the learning walks.
- push participants to be specific in their feedback. For example, when someone says, "Students are engaged," ask them, "What does 'engaged' look like or sound like?"
- design the teams.
- set the schedule.
- facilitate the debrief.
- determine how to share feedback.
- help make generalizations.
- continue to build and foster relationships within a team.

This list feels like a lot! Let's start with the first part—planning and preparing the team for learning walks.

LEARNING WALKS IN ACTION: GETTING READY

In the days or weeks leading up to the learning walk, it can be helpful to engage in the following steps so that the team is prepared for the day of the visits:

STEP 1 Select who to visit and who will be visiting

STEP 2 Introduce learning walks to the team

STEP 3 Set a focus for the visits

STEP 4 Practice making low-inference observations

These steps will set the stage for the day of the learning walk and will help make the team comfortable. Although preparing takes some time at the start,

once you have conducted walks with a team, you will not need to lay as much groundwork for future learning walks.

As you read through the specifics of each of these steps, you may find the Learning Walks Planning Template in Appendix 4 and on the 6 Tools website to be helpful. I like to use it to sketch out my plan for the walks before I begin.

STEP 1 Select Who to Visit and Who Will Be Visiting

As you begin planning for your learning walks, you need to think about where you will conduct them. For example, if you are working with a district team, you might do all your learning walks in one school, or you can do them at several schools. If you are a school-based coach, you might want to stick to your school or team up with a nearby school to do learning walks in each other's buildings. Each of these options offers benefits. In one case, you get to learn deeply about one school and see similarities and differences within the school. In the other, you are able to see how students are thinking across different schools and discuss patterns across the sites.

You also need to consider which classrooms to visit and who will be on the teams visiting. Your selections should be aligned to your goals that you have developed with your teams. For example, you may be interested in a certain content area, such as the development of fractional understanding. In that case, it would make sense to visit grades 3, 4, and 5 to see how the concept is being developed in each grade. Or, if your team wants to focus on inequities in participation, you might choose to visit a range of grade levels to see if you notice patterns in how students engage as they move through your school. In addition, it can be helpful to rotate the teachers doing the learning walks and the teachers being visited. When you first conduct walks with teams, you may want to choose teachers who are comfortable being vulnerable and are open to having their rooms visited. You can have a private conversation with them and assure them that this is a learning experience focused on students, and that the team is going to learn so much from listening to the students in the room. As you continue to do the walks, other teachers may see the process as less threatening and become more comfortable with it.

The role of the administrator is a bit trickier. The question of administrator participation comes down to the culture of your school or district. Initially, I try to conduct the learning walks with teachers alone, which allows us to be a bit more vulnerable with one another at the start and get comfortable with the process. However, I encourage administrators to join some of these walks later, because it is important to have them in classrooms in capacities other than as evaluators and be part of the learning team. I have had great success when teachers see their principal as learning along with them, which means I need to be clear with the administrator on the goals of the learning walk and ask them to take off their principal hat. Knowing the teachers and administrators in your building will allow you to strategize the best way to conduct the walks in your school or district.

STEP 2 Introduce Learning Walks to the Team

As you begin sessions with teams, it's important to think about how to introduce learning walks. I often think of the rollout of a collaborative coaching tool as the hook at the start of a new math unit. The introduction should motivate the group, engage them, and leave them wanting to be part of a process. A good goal for the initial meeting is to get as many people excited about this new learning opportunity as possible. One way is to give team members some time to reflect on a positive learning experience they have had as a teacher either visiting a classroom or having their classroom visited. Let's think about how they might answer the following questions.

STOP and JOT

What are some of the best learning experiences you have had as a teacher when visiting a classroom or having your classroom visited? What were the qualities that made these experiences powerful? What do you wish visits looked like, either as a visitor or host teacher?

Teachers often tell me that the best learning opportunities are those where they saw a student using an interesting strategy, saw a new teaching technique, or received feedback from visitors about a strategy a student in their class was using that they hadn't noticed. They have brought up instances when someone has visited their class and heard a conversation in a small group that they didn't get to hear. Any of these experiences can be used to springboard into a description of learning walks. Fostering connections between learning walks and constructive learning experiences will help start the process on a positive note, which is particularly important if you have a group that has had negative experiences with classroom visits. For example, many teachers have had district or admin teams come into their room for an evaluative visit. Furthermore, in some schools, teaching is still a private endeavor. Having colleagues come into your classroom can be a scary experience, and some teachers may feel they are in a vulnerable position.

When introducing learning walks, I find it important to talk about how we are learning about the students and not judging or evaluating the teachers being visited. It's also important to reinforce this message during the walks if team members start to become evaluative. For example, in the vignette at the start of the section, some evaluative comments were made about the teacher and students in room 602 (i.e., "Students were really bored."). If this happens in your debriefs, it can be a good opportunity to push the team to talk about exactly what the students were doing and remind them that this is not a judgment of the teacher. Sometimes we talk about focusing on the specific aspects of the tasks that engaged students versus the ones that did not to reframe the conversation on the students and not the teachers.

When learning walks are introduced, it's helpful to have the group do some short readings so that the work is grounded in the literature. Reading about how others have used learning walks allows us to think about how we might use them in our situation. Some recommendations for these readings follow:

- Fisher, D., and N. Frey. 2014. "Using Teacher Learning Walks to Improve Instruction."
- Ginsberg, M. et al. 2018. "Motivation in Motion."
- Moss, C. M., & S. M. Brookhart. 2013. "A New View of Walk-Throughs."

In addition to using articles, you can also introduce learning walks through videos. You can find examples on the 6 Tools website.

After reading an article and/or watching a video, it might be helpful for team members to reflect on some guiding questions independently, in small groups, and as a whole group. Some questions you might want to use to help the team unpack the readings or videos follow.

FACILITATION QUESTIONS About Learning Walks Readings and Videos

- How might learning walks help us develop our practice?
- What processes have these other schools/districts used for conducting learning walks?
- How are learning walks similar to/different from other PD we have received?
- What concerns do we have about conducting learning walks? How might we address them?

A chalk talk or other protocol can be helpful, especially when you anticipate challenges with a particular topic or when you are concerned that a select group of individuals might dominate the conversation. The chalk talk protocol provides everyone an opportunity to participate and share their ideas before engaging in discussion with others. A chalk talk is a particularly nice tool because teachers can use it in their classrooms with students.

To facilitate a chalk talk, write each of the guiding questions on a piece of chart paper. Give each individual a marker and explain that, for ten minutes, they are not allowed to talk with anyone else. Instead, they will walk around and write on each of the charts. They can write their own thoughts about the questions, and they can respond to one another on the charts. Set a timer for ten minutes, and get started.

After the chalk talk, give teams time to summarize the conversations on each of the charts. Small groups can each take a different chart and discuss the common themes that arose and then share with the whole group. The question about concerns can be particularly important for groups who have had negative experiences. You may find it worth spending some time to address these concerns as a group and brainstorm ways to make everyone as comfortable as possible before the walks begin.

STEP 3 Set a Focus for the Visits

After you introduce learning walks, your next step is to facilitate the team's creation of goals for the initial learning walks. What will be our particular focus? It could be grounded in the mission and vision of the school, the mathematical practices, an idea that came from a reading, or something the team is interested in studying.

One group I worked with focused their learning walks on the Common Core Standards for Mathematical Practice. (Schools in non–Common Core states can often find similar process and practice standards in their own state standards or use the *Principles and Standards for School Mathematics* from NCTM [2000].) We chose SMP 3, "Construct viable arguments and critique the reasoning of others," and unpacked it as a team. We first explored what it means to justify and construct arguments across different grade bands. We then brainstormed what evidence of the practice we might see in classrooms. The following questions guided us:

- What types of things might we see students doing if they are constructing viable arguments and critiquing the reasoning of others?
- What types of things might we hear if students are constructing viable arguments and critiquing the reasoning of others?
- What types of things might we see or hear that capture how students are supported linguistically in the lesson?
- What missed opportunities might we want to capture?

For example, we might hear students convincing a partner why their solution works. We might see a student using a drawing to explain to the class how they got their solution. We might record that a student shared a solution with the class but did not share how they knew. I like to focus the visits on trying to answer a question, so in this case, we narrowed down the question to: "How are students at this school justifying and critiquing the reasoning of others?" Our goal during the visits was to begin to answer this question.

In addition to using math practice and process standards, I have also found the Illustrative Mathematics (IM) Implementation Reflection Tool by Shelby Danks, Jennifer Wilson, Max Ray-Riek, Kristin Gray, and Kevin Liner (2021) helpful in determining a focus for walks, whether or not the school is using the IM curriculum. In particular, it includes indicators that are related to "student

The *IM Implementation Reflection Tool (Grades K–5)*

Revised: May, 2021

Part C3. Student Learning Behaviors

Students demonstrate engagement and belonging to the learning community via effective independent and collaborative problem-solving, communication of mathematical ideas, and productive struggle.

Indicator	Descriptor	Receiving	Reacting	Interacting	Belonging
C3.1 Student Independent Problem-Solving	*When assigned independent activities, most students engage in problem-solving and make their thinking visible.*	When assigned independent activities, most students **engage in unrelated activities, or wait for the teacher to share the answers.**	When assigned independent activities, most students **need teacher reminders or support** to engage in the activity.	When assigned independent activities, most students **engage in the activity, requiring little to no reminders or teacher support.**	When assigned independent activities, most students **enthusiastically take initiative to make their thinking visible, so that others can clearly understand their work.**
C3.2 Student Collaborative Problem-Solving	*When assigned collaborative work activities, students listen to each other and share their thinking throughout all stages of the problem-solving process.*	When assigned collaborative activities, **students let other students take over** the work and the thinking. Students **may work independently** when assigned paired or group tasks.	When assigned collaborative activities, **students listen to other students' solutions or ideas** and/or share their own solutions or ideas (e.g., "I got 7, what did you get?"). Students **may share** their thinking with their group **when prompted by the teacher.**	When assigned collaborative activities, students participate in **collaborative problem solving** (i.e., students talk about each other's thinking, not just their own). Students **share their thinking with their group**, and may ask the teacher for help when the group has a question rather than only when an individual has a question.	When assigned collaborative activities, students participate in collaborative problem solving (i.e., students talk about each other's thinking, not just their own), **make connections between their own strategy and others', and integrate strategies to create a group solution to a problem.** Students share their thinking **throughout multiple stages of the problem-solving process** (not just sharing solutions).
C3.3 Student Communication of Mathematical Ideas	*The students clearly communicate their mathematical ideas, both verbally or in written form.*	Students respond to verbal or written questions using **short answer responses with little explanation, even** when prompted by the teacher.	**Some students explain their thinking, verbally or in writing**, when prompted by the teacher.	Most students **extend and fully explain their reasoning (e.g., use a second sentence)**, when prompted by the teacher.	Most students fully explain their reasoning, **without being prompted by the teacher.**
C3.4 Productive Struggle *(most relevant in instances where teachers provide opportunities for productive struggle during the lesson)*	*The students know that confusion can lead to understanding, ask questions of each other, and help each other without just giving away an answer during times of difficulty, challenge, or error.*	Students **wait for help** or **do not appear to ask for help** during times of difficulty, challenge, or error.	Students **ask questions of the teacher** during times of difficulty, challenge, or error.	Students **continue working, try again, and persevere** during times of difficulty, challenge, or error. Students **may ask each other** for help when they are confused or stuck.	Students **revise their thinking and their written work includes revised explanations, added detail for making thinking visible, and justifications** after times of difficulty, challenge, or error. Students listen and help each other think through problems, **without giving away solutions.**

Figure 4.1 The "student learning behaviors" section of the Illustrative Mathematics Implementation Reflection Tool

learning behaviors" (Figure 4.1) such as problem-solving skills, communication of mathematical ideas, and productive struggle. You might share this portion of the tool with the team and have them discuss which aspects they would like to focus the learning walk on. For example, they may want to explore how students collaborate when problem solving. If so, they could look at whether students independently share their solutions with group members and make connections among their problem-solving strategies. The team may decide that when they enter the rooms, each team member will take notes on how students work together in a group on a task, recording the different strategy solutions, the ways in which students interact with each other, and the questions the teacher uses when they circulate to the group.

The Teach for the Robust Understanding of Math (TRU) framework (Schoenfeld and the Teaching for Robust Understanding Project 2016) is a third source of ideas for framing your learning walks. It was designed by researchers to focus on the following five dimensions of powerful classroom practice:

- The content
- Cognitive demand
- Equitable access to content
- Agency, ownership, and identity
- Formative assessment

These dimensions push us to think about the lesson from the student's perspective. Your team might want to take a deep dive into one of the dimensions. For example, you could focus your walks on equitable access to content. The team can explore the resources on this topic, brainstorm some indicators they might see in the classrooms, and then use the walks to answer the question: "How are students at our school given opportunities to contribute in meaningful ways?" During the walk, they might focus their notes on which students participate in the lesson and how often, the variety of opportunities students have to explain their thinking, the ways in which students have various entry points to the lesson, and how all students, including multilingual and special education students, have access to the lesson.

The Standards for Mathematical Practice (or state process and practice standards), the IM observation tool, and the TRU framework are rich places to explore as you develop a focus question for your walks. These resources are linked in the 6 Tools website so you can explore them and pinpoint which is most helpful, depending on your goals for the team. You might also use the walks as an opportunity to explore a book or article you have been reading together. Again, using what you know about your school and teams will help you determine what your focus might be. Take a minute to think about the strengths and needs of your teams and what they might benefit from.

STOP and JOT

What are some questions you might want to explore with your teams that build on their strengths and address some of their needs?

What resources might help you?

Other teams I have worked with explored questions aimed at discovering how students are

- making sense of the real world using mathematics?
- constructing viable arguments?
- engaged in productive struggle?
- learning through problem solving?
- reflecting on their learning?
- making connections between different mathematical ideas?
- using representations?

These queries help to codevelop the focus with the team. What are some ideas that the team is interested in focusing on that align with your learning goals for them? This alignment can help make the learning walks more relevant for everyone.

STEP 4 Practice Making Low-Inference Observations

Your team may have had lots of experience visiting classrooms together, or they may not be used to visiting one another's rooms with a team. In either case, developing norms for visiting classrooms, recording observations, and analyzing observations is an important step to make sure that everyone is on the same page and that the conditions exist for learning to occur among the team members. I have found that before entering classrooms, it can be helpful to use video to develop these norms, which allows me as the facilitator to address any challenges that might arise before we are in a colleagues' classroom. This norm-setting is especially helpful for groups that may not fully trust or be vulnerable with one another yet. It can be helpful to start with someone that the group doesn't know. Choose a short video clip that has recordings of both the teacher and groups of students talking. The 6 Tools website offers several options.

Before watching the video, have the team complete the math task and anticipate student responses, which allows all members of the team to have access to the mathematics the students are working on. This step also focuses the attention on mathematics and student thinking as opposed to teacher moves.

After discussing the math, you can move to introducing low-inference observations. You might give some examples and nonexamples so that the team is clear on what to record. Looking back at the statements from Tool 3: Visiting Classrooms might be helpful. For instance, have teachers contrast the following two statements:

- Students were working on a boring worksheet.
- All twenty-five students were working independently on a handout that included twenty problems in which they needed to find the common denominator of two fractions. Three students whispered "I'm bored" as I walked around the room.

Although the first statement may be true, it has an evaluative nature to it. The second statement is nonevaluative and gives detailed information that will allow us to identify specific next steps.

After practicing with a handful of examples, move to the video. As the video plays, the team takes low-inference observations about what students are saying and doing. After the team has recorded observations, it can be helpful to assess the types of notes they recorded and norm what a low-inference observation is. To do this, in either small groups or with the large group, ask participants to share all their observations and have someone record them in one visible place. The following questions can be helpful for small groups to discuss.

101

FACILITATION QUESTIONS About Low-Inference Observations

❓ Are the noticings low inference? If not, how could you change them?

❓ Are the noticings specific? Do any terms need to be further defined?

❓ What patterns do you notice?

❓ What summary statements could you write based on these patterns?

As the groups discuss and share, you can collect data on what teachers are noticing and wondering, and you can ask probing questions. For example, you might ask groups follow-up questions similar to the following sample questions.

FOLLOW-UP FACILITATION QUESTIONS About Low-Inference Observations

❓ What do you mean by "students were engaged"?

❓ What evidence do you have that students met the objective?

❓ What makes the task "high demand"?

❓ What do you think the student understood when they solved the task in that way?

We saw Ms. James do some of this earlier. Asking teachers to define certain terms they are using, such as "engaged" or "understanding," can help clarify what they mean by these terms.

Here's another example from a debrief I recently led:

Mr. C: The students understand how to add positive and negative numbers.

Me: How do we know that?

Mr. C: All the students' work showed they added −5 + 7 correctly.

Me: Do we know how they know that?

Mr. C: Two of the students told me the rule.

Me: Do we know if they know why the rule works?

Ms. L: I don't think so. Because when the teacher asked the group to show why the answer was 2, they didn't have any other way than the rule.

Me: So, what do we think they understand and not understand?

Mr. C: They know the procedure but don't necessarily know why it works.

Ms. L: It seems like they might need some help understanding why the rule works in case they forget it.

Me: Interesting . . . I wonder what some other implications could be.

By pushing the team to be specific about what students understand, I was able to open up an interesting conversation about the different types of "understanding" students might demonstrate.

When the share is complete, summarize the discussion and create an agreed-upon set of norms for taking low-inference notes that you will use during the learning walks.

LEARNING WALKS IN ACTION: THE DAY OF THE LEARNING WALK

Now that you've oriented the team to learning walks, set a focus for visits, and practiced taking low-inference notes with videos, you are all ready to head out to classrooms. During these initial learning walks, the team will practice and develop their skills and continue to develop norms. The following steps can help organize the team the day of the learning walk:

STEP 1 Engage with the math before heading out

STEP 2 Visit the classrooms

STEP 3 Debrief the learning walk

Make sure to schedule your learning walks so you have enough processing time throughout: you'll need a little time to engage in the math tasks, review norms, and talk about the schedule before you set out; time to visit and have quick talks between classrooms; and some debrief time after all your visits. I find the whole learning walk process usually takes between two and three hours, not including the prework described earlier, which I usually do in separate team meetings or professional development time prior to the day of the walk. I try to keep the classroom visits to one hour and then give the team anywhere between one and two hours to debrief. I find that you need closer to three hours when you start to develop the norms for the debrief process. After several rounds, the debrief takes less time.

Let's take a look at how things might flow on the day of the learning walks.

STEP 1 Engage with the Math Before Heading Out

If possible, before heading out, take a few minutes to look at the task the students will be working on and anticipate responses before going into classes. This step takes a little extra planning but allows the team to really think about the task and anticipate how students might respond to it. Patterns might start to emerge about the types of tasks, and it's important to record these somewhere. Google Docs or chart paper are simple ways to capture the learning about the tasks so that you can come back to these ideas when you debrief later. If you can provide coverage for the teachers you will be visiting so they can meet with the team, a quick conversation can be invaluable. The teacher can share how they planned the lesson and what the team will be seeing, which provides insight into what the goals of the lesson are.

STEP 2 Visit the Classrooms

As you prepare to head out to classrooms, share the schedule of the rooms the team will be going to visit. I recommend spending fifteen minutes each in three classrooms. The following protocol is helpful in organizing the team.

CLASSROOM VISIT PROTOCOL

- We split the room into sections, and each person takes notes on a different section of students.
- We record low-inference observations about what the students are thinking, doing, and saying.
- When we leave each room, we spend five to ten minutes doing a quick round-robin share of what we noticed and what we wondered related to our focus. We try to find an area away from the teachers' classroom for these conversations—an empty classroom, a spot in the hall on another floor, or the library. (Huddling right outside the teacher's room can sometimes feel a little intimidating to the teacher who was just visited.)
- After all the classroom visits are complete, we debrief.

I have found groups of three or four to be ideal for classroom visits. A small number is not too overwhelming for the teachers, but there are enough of us to each focus on a different section of students. When I have large groups, we still try to stay in groups of three or four, but we rotate rooms so that one group goes into classroom A, a second group goes into classroom B, and a third group goes into classroom C, and then we rotate every fifteen minutes. During the round-robin share, you might want to jot down notes to bring up when you do the full debrief, and you can strategically share things you noticed and wondered if the group does not bring them up. When you do learning walks with larger groups and cannot be with each team, try to select team leaders for each group who can record key observations and keep the group on task.

During the classroom visits, your role is to keep time and handle logistics and also to take low-inference notes as an observer alongside your team. You can make periodic reminders that participants should put the classroom teachers at ease and focus on student learning, rather than teacher moves. Be sure to thank hosting teachers as you circulate.

STEP 3 Debrief the Learning Walk

After all the teams visit all three classrooms, it's time to analyze the data. The goals of the analysis are to (1) begin to answer the guiding question and (2) brainstorm next steps. When I first started doing debriefs after learning walks, I didn't follow a particular protocol or structure. We all discussed what we saw when we came back and then developed next steps. Sometimes this casual style worked well, and sometimes it didn't. When it didn't work well, it was often because the discussions were dominated by one or two pieces of evidence that the team found most salient. As a result, we often missed a lot of the data that was collected during our visits. Over time, I started using a more structured debrief protocol so we could look at our data more systematically.

DEBRIEF PROTOCOL

- Individually organize the data
- Analyze the group's data
- Reflect and create next steps

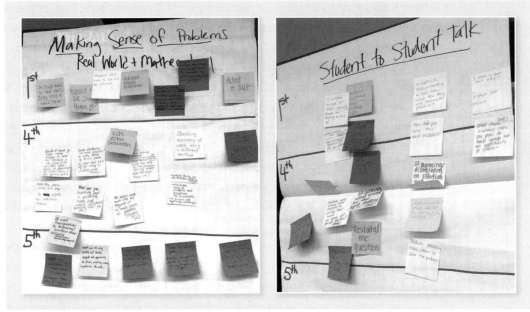

Figure 4.2 (left) Evidence of students making sense of problems
Figure 4.3 (right) Evidence of student-to-student talk

Individually Organize the Data

As soon as you finish the walks, give participants independent time, which helps focus the conversation on the data and what people observed students doing and saying, before the group discussion. Ask each person to look at their notes and record at least three statements for each classroom on sticky notes. Encourage them to write a separate note for every new statement. Look over your own notes and strategically select the pieces of data that you want to highlight and record those on sticky notes as well.

After a few minutes, collect these notes on chart paper. You can see in the pictures in Figures 4.2 and 4.3 how a team of coaches and I collected evidence of students making sense of problems and student-to-student talk, and then we separated notes into the grade levels we visited.

Analyze the Group's Data

After gathering all the sticky notes, start to look for patterns. What does the team notice about the observations you collected? What patterns emerge? What questions do you have? If I am doing this activity with a small team of four or five, we work through this together. We usually have about twelve sticky notes for each classroom, which allows us to notice any patterns. If I have larger groups, say, three groups of five, I often split up the notes by classrooms and then ask each group to focus on analyzing the combined data from one of the classrooms.

As we look through the sticky notes, we develop some summary statements that help answer our question. The most important part of this step is that we ground the statements in evidence. For example, if we noticed that, in two out of three classrooms we visited, the students were engaged in problem solving, it's important to clarify what we mean by "engaged in problem solving" and what our evidence is for saying that. I find it helps to keep asking the team additional questions to get at the details. For example:

- What types of problems were students solving?
- Were they solving them by themselves or in groups?
- What does *active student engagement* mean? Does it mean that they were thinking hard about the problems or that they were being compliant and solving the problems?

This step isn't easy. We can organize the data in many different ways and might notice or wonder about many different things. For example, see Figure 4.4 for one example of how teachers analyzed data about students making sense of problems.

It's OK to organize the data in different ways: the goal is to create a list of initial patterns and wonderings, and you might investigate some of these questions later. You also want to notice how students are reasoning about particular mathematical content. For example, what strategies did students use to reason about fraction addition? What strategies did they use to add numbers? What different understandings did you notice about these topics?

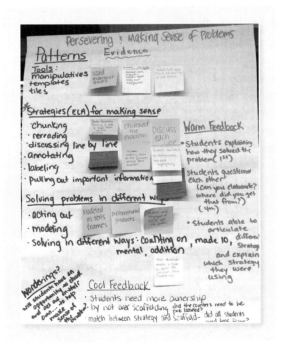

Figure 4.4 Teams analyze their data.

ANALYZING DATA: LET'S TRY IT

Below are some sticky notes collected from a learning walk in a classroom where students were working in stations, solving the following problem. Before reading on, you may want to stop and do the problem yourself and anticipate the different ways students might solve it.

A teacher buys 8 packs of orange erasers and 6 packs of blue erasers for his classroom. There are 24 orange erasers in a pack and 28 blue erasers in a pack. What is the total number of erasers the teacher buys for his classroom?

The focus of the learning walk was "How are students making sense of problems?" As you look through the following summary statements, answer the following questions: What do you notice? What patterns emerge? What questions do you have?

Students who struggled at two tables were given highlighters and told to highlight the important information. They highlighted the entire problem.

After being given five minutes to think about the problem individually, students turned and talked with a partner about their solution.

A pair of students circled 24 and 28 and added them together to get 52.

Students at table 5 read the problem, circled the numbers and the word "total," and added the four numbers. When I asked why they added, they said "because total means to add."

A student shared her solution with the class by drawing eight circles with the number 24 in them and then drawing six circles with the number 28 in them.

Student asked another student: "Where did you get 32,256 from?"

"I used multiplication. That's what we did yesterday."

A student successfully solved the problem by multiplying 8 and 24 and then 6 and 28 and then adding the products. When I asked how she arrived at her solution, she said, "I pictured the story in my head, and I knew that that there would be 8 groups of 24 erasers and 6 groups of 28 erasers so I could multiply 8 times 24 or I could add 24+24+24+24+24+24+24+24, but that would take a while. And then I could multiply 6 and 28 and then add the answers."

Students did not have any manipulatives available at their tables.

FIVE STUDENTS FINISHED THE PROBLEM QUICKLY AND WAITED FOR THE REST OF THE GROUP TO FINISH.

STOP and JOT

 Take a moment to answer the following questions before reading about our team's ideas:

- What do you notice?
- What patterns emerge?
- What questions do you have?

Here are some of the patterns that we noticed:

- Drawing a picture and visualizing the problem in terms of "groups of" led to successful solutions.
- Students who relied on a keyword strategy were not successful.
- Students were given opportunities to explore the problem on their own and time to talk with a partner.
- Students who struggled were still not successful when using the highlighters that were provided as an intervention.

Here are some of the questions we asked. You may have additional questions to add.

- How could we use some students' strategies of drawing and visualizing groups to help the rest of the class?
- What could students who finish early do to be challenged?
- How might physical manipulatives help students make sense of problems when they don't know how to start?

We engaged in this same process for the other classrooms, and then we looked across the classrooms to see what patterns emerged.

As the team works through this protocol, facilitate the conversation so you can engage the group in reviewing the data and start conversations about what students are learning and how learning is fostered or could be better fostered. I find it helps to be the recorder during this facilitation. Recording forces me to take a step back and also allows me to push the team to be specific in their creation of these statements.

After the team has had time to notice patterns and develop questions, invite the hosting classroom teachers to join the group so participants can share. When I facilitate learning walks, I wait until the very end to bring the class-room teachers in because I really want the observing teachers to think about what they noticed students doing and saying. When the classroom teachers are brought in, they often feel the need to explain their instructional decisions to their colleagues. Although this reflection is interesting and valuable, it can take the focus off student learning. As a result, I have found it most helpful to bring the teachers in at the end and have the observers share our final notic-ings and wonderings about student learning with them. Then, we all reflect and create next steps for the team together.

Reflect and Next Steps

After debriefing but before disbanding, it's important for the team to reflect on the process and what they learned from participating in it. Some prompts to help guide these individual reflections follow.

FACILITATION QUESTIONS to Reflect on Learning Walks

? Think about your classroom and how you can apply what we learned here to your students. What would be some next steps for you? Include one next step that you can try out immediately (this week or next) in your classroom.

? Reflect on the summary statements and next steps. What are some next steps for our learning as a team?

After team members reflect individually for a few minutes, they can share what they learned and brainstorm next steps. During this debrief, the group can review the questions they developed and determine which of them they want to explore further in the next learning walk as well as what types of professional learning they might want to engage in. For example, the team may decide to start a book club related to one of the questions they noticed.

After the team has finished for the day, it's important for you to take some time to reflect on the learning walks, the group dynamics, what you think the team learned, and what some next steps for you are—as a coach. What went well? What might you clarify or tweak for next time? While the day is still fresh in your mind, you might strategically form teams for the next learning walk. We need to learn from different individuals, and as the purpose of the walks changes, the groupings can change as well. You can also think about who visited which classrooms, which classrooms were visited, and which classrooms would make sense to visit next. Although there is always something to learn from all classroom visits about student thinking, certain classrooms allow for different opportunities. In addition, it is also a good time to think about the connections to your individual coaching work. Are there specific things that came out of the walk and debrief that you want to focus on with an individual teacher? Did a teacher specifically mention an idea they want to try out? The conversations that arise during the learning walks can be a nice springboard for you to work one-on-one with teachers.

THE OUTCOME: FOCUSING THE TEAM ON STUDENTS' THINKING

Doing learning walks well takes a lot of time, and time is one resource we never have enough of. However, spending the time to help teachers collaboratively develop a deep understanding about what it means to teach and learn mathematics is more effective than spending time bombarding them with a number of "new" instructional strategies. The learning that occurs from this process is long-lasting and has the potential to change teachers' understanding of what it means to examine and improve instruction at a school.

For example, one theme that emerges often is that students are capable of far greater mathematical thinking than we give them credit for. On many learning walks I have heard teachers say, "I never thought of solving the problem that way," or "The teacher didn't teach him that yet. How did he know how to do it?" This realization happens because, during learning walks, we can just listen to kids. We don't have the pressure of anticipating our next teaching move or worrying about whether the students at table 5 are on task. I often hear from teachers how much they enjoy the opportunity to step away from their role as the teacher, to sit back and watch students learn during the learning walk. Max Ray-Riek does a great job of talking about why listening *to* students is more important than listening *for* answers in his short Ignite talk, "Why 2 is greater than 4: A Proof by Induction" (2011). It's shared on the 6 Tools website, and you may want to watch it with your teacher teams to further develop this idea.

The next step is to start to apply what we are learning about student thinking from our interviews and learning walks to our teaching practice. In the next tool, we will explore how to use routines and rehearsals with your teacher teams.

REFLECTING on LEARNING

- What skills do you have that will help you facilitate the learning walks? What skills do you need to develop? How will you do this?

- What team needs do you anticipate as you implement learning walks?

- Look at the analysis charts in Figures 4.2–4.4. What do you notice/wonder about them? What questions might you ask to push the thinking of the group?

- Call to action: write a plan for how you might modify the learning walk protocols outlined to meet the needs in your school(s).

EXPLORING the LITERATURE

The research literature shows many benefits to teachers conducting structured visits to classrooms. Learning walks lend themselves to opportunities for teams to have thoughtful and productive conversations about teaching and learning (Ginsberg and Murphy 2002; Fisher and Frey 2014; Kachur, Stout, and Edwards 2010, 2013; Stephens 2011).

However, simply visiting classrooms is not enough. In fact, if visits are not done thoughtfully, they can be harmful to goals of improving teacher learning. Kachur and colleagues (2013) have noted that visits need to have certain aspects to be productive. These aspects include:

- Setting a clear purpose of the visit and focused look-fors
- Communicating feedback
- Framing the process as formative and reflective as opposed to summative and evaluative.

The conversation that occurs after these visits is also important and should focus on using evidence to make sense of student thinking and classroom events. Researchers have found that protocol-based conversations have a positive impact when they are focused on a clear purpose and held in a respectful and collegial environment (Selkrig and Keamy 2015). Learning walks are one way to allow for these opportunities.

REHEARSING ROUTINES
Practicing with Colleagues

Paul, a first-year teacher, is standing at a large white board that has 16 x 25 written on it. "Give me a silent thumb when you have a solution. If you have more than one solution, show me with your other fingers how many different ways you could solve it."

The rest of the fourth-grade team is sitting around him, acting as students. In previous team meetings, we read articles about Number Talks and watched videos of other teachers conducting them. Today, we were rehearsing Number Talks during our professional development time.

After two minutes, Paul says, "OK. What solutions do we have?"

"400." One teacher calls out. Other teachers nod in agreement.

"OK. Are there any other answers?"

"230." I say.

"OK. Any other answers?"

No one answers.

"Great. Nicora, why don't we start with yours? How did you get 230?"

"Can we pause for a second?" Rory, one of the team members asks. "I want to know why you chose the wrong answer to start with."

"I was thinking that it might be easier to hear about Nicora's thinking early on and then see if we could figure out how to address it," Paul replies.

"Interesting. I think I would have picked the right answers and then asked Nicora if she wanted to change her mind after she heard it," Rory says.

"I was worried that she might just change it once she heard someone else, and we wouldn't know why she changed it or what she was thinking," Paul answers.

I jump in at this point. "I think this is one of those places where we can make different decisions. There doesn't seem to be one right way to do this—each will have advantages and disadvantages. We don't want students to learn that whichever solution is chosen first is always the right one or the wrong one, so we are going to have to vary our response. I think you could make an argument for calling on either solution to start as long as we continue to vary it. Let's go back to the problem and see how Paul's choice plays out."

"Nicora, can you explain how you got 230?" Paul asks.

"I used partial products. I did 6 times 5 which is equal to 30 and then 10 times 20 which is equal to 200, and then I added 200 + 30 together." I explain, pretending to have a common student conception.

Paul records my thinking on the board (Figure 5.1) and says, "Interesting. But I think you forgot to do all the partial products. Can you figure out which ones you missed?"

"No. I did them all."

Paul pauses. "Hmmm . . . can someone else who did partial products but got a different answer share their thinking?"

We paused the Number Talk here again and at several other points where we had different questions about the choices we could make. For example, we talked about the ways Paul represented student thinking and whether we should give students a chance to turn and talk at different points. We debriefed, and then a different teacher took on the role of the teacher with a different problem.

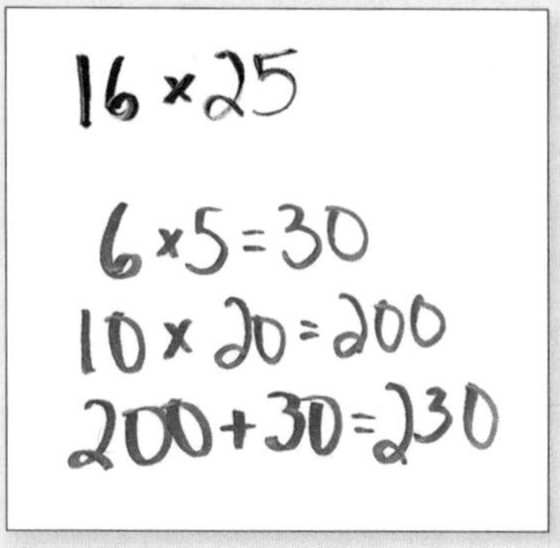

$$16 \times 25$$

$$6 \times 5 = 30$$
$$10 \times 20 = 200$$
$$200 + 30 = 230$$

Figure 5.1
Number Talk recording

HOW CAN WE DEVELOP OUR COACHING SKILLS THROUGH REHEARSING ROUTINES?

Instructional routines such as Number Talks (Humphreys and Parker 2015, Parrish 2022) have a specific format that repeats so students know what to expect. Using them regularly has the potential to build mathematical thinking habits (Kelemanik, Lucenta, and Creighton 2016). From a coaching point of view, not only do these routines benefit students in classrooms but the rehearsals of routines with teacher teams, as we saw in the vignette, can be a great strategy to add to your coaching toolbox.

STOP and JOT

What did you notice about the rehearsal of a routine in the opening vignette? What was the role of the coach? What learning opportunities existed for the team?

You may have noticed that when *rehearsing routines*, one team member leads an instructional activity while the others role-play the students. Rehearsals provide opportunities for teams to work together to practice a particular instructional strategy, discuss their decision making, and develop their skills in eliciting and responding to student thinking before they try the routine with their own students.

My use of routines and rehearsals as a coach was inspired by the work of Magdalene Lampert and colleagues (2013) and Elham Kazemi and colleagues (2016), who have used and studied rehearsals extensively in mathematics teacher education. I began exploring the implementation and rehearsal of different instructional routines when I was struggling with moving from teacher-directed to student-centered lessons. Originally, I would work with teams on planning an

117

entire lesson that was student-centered, which quickly became overwhelming for teachers. I would hear comments like: "How can I do this *every* day?" "When will students have time to practice skills?" "But what about preparing them for the test?" and "Do we have to rewrite every lesson in the textbook?"

When we were planning a full lesson, we needed to think about a hook, what tasks to use or modify, what questions support student thinking, how to differentiate, how to facilitate a whole-class summary, how to assess and monitor progress, and so on. Taking all of this on can feel like a lot and can seem like you are asking a team to try to change everything all at once. Think of a teacher you work with who has a very teacher-directed classroom. Trying to work with that teacher and have them switch all their lessons to a more student-based approach can seem insurmountable. In addition, changing all aspects of math instruction at once invalidates everything the teacher is currently doing. Now think about working on a five- to fifteen-minute routine with that teacher—a routine that they can incorporate into their current math block. Does focusing on this one piece seem more manageable for both the teacher and you? It does for me. In fact, I find that routines can be a great entry point for teacher teams that I am struggling with in terms of shifting practice. Rehearsing and enacting routines supports teachers in making small shifts in their practice that yield big results— results that have everyday impact and feel doable for them. And it doesn't take long for these shifts to spill out past the five- to fifteen-minute routine, into the rest of the math block.

When I started working with routines, starting with such a small part of the lesson felt like taking baby steps when we had so much big work to do, but I've learned that both routines and rehearsals quickly become compelling for coaches and teachers because they allow us to zoom in on student thinking during our teaching. Teaching is so complex, and it can be hard to simplify it in a way that still honors the complexities of the work. The format of a predictable routine, however, allows us to foreground certain parts—like student thinking— and background others—like the structure and flow of the whole lesson. The routine still allows for complex questions and discussions to arise; it just narrows the focus of these discussions to a small slice of instruction. Routines also help me focus my coaching: we can use our planning time to anticipate and record responses or analyze questions that push students' thinking.

If we're going to implement instructional routines, the next question becomes, what's the best way to prepare teachers to teach them? Some teachers might say that reading an article or watching a video is enough for them to get a sense of the routine and teach it, but I'd argue that rehearsing the routines together is where the real coaching value lies. Rehearsing routines allows the team members to become comfortable opening up their practice to each other. They can take risks in rehearsals that they might not feel comfortable trying in the classroom. Teachers also have the opportunity to explore different strategies that students might use to solve the problems. Rehearsals allow us to look at routines across different grade levels, incorporate them into any current program or curriculum, and then think about bigger changes from there.

Rehearsing routines together was something I originally learned about when I was working with preservice teachers, and at first, I was worried that more experienced teacher teams might find it silly or feel reluctant to rehearse a routine in front of a group of their peers. However, I found that veteran teachers often appreciate the opportunity to try out a new routine with their colleagues before trying it with a class. They also respond to the collaborative element of rehearsals and enjoy that we are all planning, practicing, and giving feedback together. With team after team, I've found that rehearsing and enacting routines together is a powerful way to build collaborative team and school culture, maybe especially when the members of the team have varying levels of experience and knowledge.

REHEARSING ROUTINES IN ACTION

When thinking about how to use routines and rehearsals with teacher teams, I was greatly influenced by researchers and teacher educators such as Magdalene Lampert, Elham Kazemi, Hala Ghousseini, Megan Franke, and others who work with novice teachers at the University of Michigan, the University of Washington, and UCLA. You can read more about their work at tedd.org, which you can access from the 6 Tools website. I adapted their structures for inservice teachers, shown here, but feel free to modify the steps for your team.

STEP 1 Choose a routine

STEP 2 Learn about the routine

STEP 3 Plan and rehearse the routine

STEP 4 Implement the routine with students

STEP 5 Reflect and plan next steps

Throughout these steps, your role as the coach is to facilitate the learning and set norms for feedback so that you are supporting and nurturing a risk-taking environment.

As you read through the specifics of each of these steps, you may find the Rehearsing Routines Planning Template in Appendix 5 and on the 6 Tools website to be helpful. I like to use it to sketch out my learning plan for the team before I begin the work. As with a lesson plan for students, you can modify and adjust it based on the needs of the team. You may find it helpful to jot ideas down on it as you read through the different steps.

STEP 1 Choose a Routine

Choosing a routine depends on your team's goals, where they are as learners and teachers, and how you think you can best support them as a coach. Some teams might have more experience with routines than others. New teachers might benefit from simpler routines, whereas experienced teachers may be ready to take on more complex routines. Some routines might fit better into certain programs/curricula than others. Think about your goals for your team as well as the current strengths that they have as you figure out which routines to use.

Also, take teachers' interests into account. For example, if the team is interested in learning how to help students understand story problems, focus on a routine related to this type of problem, like the Three Reads routine or Numberless Word Problems. If they are learning how to help students develop number sense and fluency, maybe Number Talks or Choral Counting are the right choices. To give the team some agency and ownership of the routine selection, you could present two or three routines to choose from, and they can decide which one they would like to start with. This process allows you to control and vet the quality of the routines that they can choose from, but it allows the team to make a final decision on which routine might best suit their students.

It's important to choose routines that have a clear structure that repeats and that allows us to see and hear a range of student thinking. Then, during rehearsal and enactment, we can focus on how we listen to students' thinking, probe their thinking, and respond to it in the moment. As the coach, I can ask facilitation questions that steer the conversation to student thinking. Similar to when we do learning walks or conduct student interviews, we want to foreground the student thinking. Teacher moves will still come up but in service of helping us elicit and respond to student thinking.

I have found the routines in Table 5.1 particularly useful in my work with teacher teams. You might have others to add to your list. Online resources are linked on the 6 Tools website.

Table 5.1 Recommended instructional routines

ROUTINE	DESCRIPTION	FURTHER RESOURCES
Number Talks 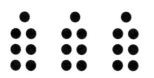	Students solve problems mentally and discuss their strategies while a teacher represents their thinking.	*Number Talks: Whole Number Computation* (2022), *Number Talks: Fraction, Decimals, and Percentages* (2022), *Making Number Talks Matter* (2015), *Digging Deeper: Making Number Talks Matter Even More* (2018)
Quick Images How many dots do you see? How do you see them?	Students are shown an image of groups of objects for a few seconds and are asked how many there are in order to develop their understanding of quantity.	*Number Talks: Whole Number Computation* (2022), *Number Sense Routines: Building Numerical Literacy Every Day in Grades K–3* (2011), *Number Sense Routines: Building Mathematical Understanding Every Day in Grades 3–5* (2018), *Early Childhood Math Routines* (2020)
How Many? 	Students decide what to count in an image with multiple possibilities.	*How Many?* (2018)

ROUTINE	DESCRIPTION	FURTHER RESOURCES
Which One Doesn't Belong? 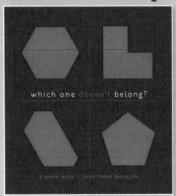	Students examine four shapes, numbers, or graphs and find a reason why one doesn't belong. These tasks are designed in such a way that there can be a reason for each item not to belong, which means students need to justify their reasoning.	*Which One Doesn't Belong?* (2016) and www.wodb.ca.
Notice and Wonder 	Students are shown an image, video, or mathematical scenario and are asked what they notice and what they wonder about it.	*Powerful Problem Solving* (2013) and https://www.nctm.org/noticeandwonder/
Estimation 180	Students view images or brief videos and make estimations about the quantities in them. Images often build upon one another, so students can use what they learned from a previous image to improve their estimation skills on the next image.	https://estimation180.com/

ROUTINE	DESCRIPTION	FURTHER RESOURCES
Numberless Word Problems 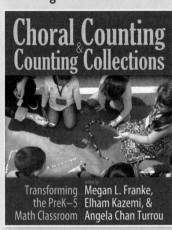	Students explore contextual problems that do not include numbers, which allows them to make sense of the scenario and the structure of a problem before performing any calculations.	https://bstockus.word-press.com/number-less-word-problems/ and https://hcpss.instructure.com/courses/107/pages/numberless-word-problems
Choral Counting and Counting Collections	Students count aloud together and notice patterns in the counting sequences during Choral Counts. In Counting Collections, students are given collections of items (paper clips, buttons, rubber bands, etc.) to organize, count, and represent.	*Choral Counting and Counting Collections* (2018)

The next set of resources are compilations of related routines:

■ *High-Yield Routines for Grades K–8* (2013). This book describes seven different routines to use in classrooms. One routine I have found particularly useful in my work is Today's Number, where students are asked to represent the number of the day using various methods such as concrete materials, drawings, or equations. The other routine I use often is Alike and Different, where students are shown two images, numbers, expressions, equations, or graphs and find what is the same and what is different between them. These other sites are also useful for same and different images: https://samedifferentimages.wordpress.com/ and https://www.samebutdifferentmath.com.

- *Routines for Reasoning: Fostering The Mathematical Practices in All Students* (2016). *Routines for Reasoning* pays special attention to how high-quality routines address different learners in the classroom, including multilingual students and students with special needs. The Three Reads routine in the book has been the most popular in the schools I have worked with, because teachers have found it helps their students make sense of word problems.
- www.tedd.org. Finally, The Teacher Education by Design (TEDD) site is a comprehensive resource for routines and how to use them with teacher teams. It has videos of various routines, as well as planning and debriefing templates and protocols that are useful. Many of the routines mentioned earlier are described in more detail on this site.

Asking a team to commit to doing a routine with their class several times a week for one month has been helpful. Depending on the routine, the frequency might change. For example, Counting Collections takes more time and might be better suited to using once a week, whereas Number Talks can be implemented two or three times per week. Regardless, trying out the routine for a month allows us to become comfortable with it, gather some data, and analyze where we are. Also, asking the group to commit to something for one month is less intimidating than thinking we have to use it forever. And I have found that once we really commit to it and try it out regularly, teachers want to keep doing it, or the team wants to try out more routines to add to our repertoire.

Often initiatives fail because we ask people to commit to something for the long term, and we don't allow room for design changes. Instead, it can be more productive to say, "Let's pilot this and then see what is working and what is not. We can change course if we need to." Either way, we've learned something about student thinking, and we can reflect on what we've learned and how it might impact our instruction. We may have only conquered five to fifteen minutes of the lesson, but we have opened conversations and become more willing to try out new ideas. These small steps can yield big returns later.

STEP 2 Learn About the Routine

Now that you and the team have decided on a routine, it's time to dive deeper and learn more about it. I recommend finding an article, blog post, or chapter on the routine that you can all read, so you'll have a grounding text to refer to as you rehearse. In addition to reading about the routine, it's really helpful for teachers to watch the routine in action before trying it out. I recommend using a video so that you can be strategic. Search for one in the resources about routines, or record yourself or another teacher implementing the routine. (As I mentioned earlier, a great resource for finding videos is https://tedd.org/mathematics/. The site includes information about the videos, as well as sample plans for analyzing and debriefing the videos with teams.) Once you've chosen your video, you can plan what you want to focus the team's attention on, when you might want to pause the video to ask questions, and what questions to ask that will foster the team's learning. Here are some sample general questions that you might consider asking; however, also think about questions that are specific to the routine you choose.

FACILITATION QUESTIONS for Watching Videos or Reading About Routines

? What do you notice about the routine?

? How does the routine allow us to learn about student thinking? What questions does the teacher ask that uncover student thinking?

? What challenges do you anticipate? How might we address them?

As you facilitate these discussions, you may find that the team is interested in how the routines will work within their classrooms given their students, schedules, and current curriculum. For example, you may want to decide as a team what components of the math period might need to be adjusted to make time for the routine. Could the routine replace a current warm-up? Could the routine be used during morning meeting? You also might discuss how to adapt the routines for different learners, such as by providing sentence frames for emerging bilingual or multilingual students. It may also be important to determine the role of special education, English language, or intervention teachers during the routines.

These conversations about modifying routines to meet the needs of the students in the schools in which you are working are important and address a concern I initially had about routines, which was whether they were too scripted and too rigid. All too often I have seen teachers handed curriculums that they felt confined by and that didn't take their expertise into account. I was concerned that introducing a routine wouldn't allow teachers to be flexible and to respond to student thinking in the moment. However, I found that the predictable structures of the routines actually allow teachers a greater ability to listen to student thinking and respond to it.

Routines are not a script to follow. Instead, routines help students and teachers know what to expect while still allowing teachers to add their flair. Teachers can adapt the routines to their style and modify them in ways that work for their classrooms. I like to think of the routine as a basic recipe, rather than a prescriptive one. We need some consistent ingredients and ratios between them so the cake rises, but sometimes we may add different flavors or twists to it. Routines give us a basic recipe for exploring student thinking. The more we practice, the more we learn whether the batter is too sticky or too dry. Then, we can add our own touch while keeping true to our goals. So, when we discuss the routines, we want to talk about which things will stay the same for all classrooms and which things we might change or add. This process gives us a sense of what it feels like to open up an activity to allow student thinking to shine.

STEP 3 Plan and Rehearse the Routine

After studying the routine and discussing it, we move to sketching out mini–lesson plans for the routine in our grade teams. During this step, I encourage the team to anticipate as many student responses as they can. Sometimes we do this preparation in the same session in which we watched the video; sometimes it is during the following session. In either case, after teams have had some collaborative work time, we share our planning decisions and provide a bit of feedback. I don't spend too much time giving feedback at this point because the rehearsals will allow us to give plenty of that and make revisions, but a few minutes enables us to set the expectation that we'll be asking questions of and responding to one another.

Next, each team chooses one person to rehearse the routine. One of our important roles as a coach at this point is to set norms, including how we will behave as students, how and when we will interrupt the rehearsal if we have questions, and what type of feedback will be helpful after we complete the routine. It can also be useful to remind the group that the main focus of these rehearsals is to examine the different student strategies that arise. Once the norms are set, it can be important to reinforce them throughout the rehearsals. For example, let's say the group has set norms about what it means to act as students. They have decided that it does not mean that we will mimic behaviors that a fourth grader might display socially but rather that we will anticipate how fourth graders might answer. Then during the rehearsal, if one of the team members starts saying things like, "My fourth graders would be throwing pencils at each other now," you can redirect the conversation and remind everyone of the agreed-upon norms. Although we absolutely should discuss engagement during the debrief, we want to maintain focus first on the different strategies students might use. Thinking about strategies allows us to see whether our task is open-ended enough, helps us build our bank of anticipated strategies, and provides opportunities to rehearse how we might respond to different strategies. Therefore, you may want to focus explicitly on strategies at the start and promise the team that there will be a time to talk about engagement at the end.

It's also important to set norms about how we give feedback to the team member who is rehearsing the routine. We want to give input that is focused on the students. You may want to look back at Tool 4 and think about reviewing or connecting to some of the feedback norms from Learning Walks when you are rehearsing the routines.

One question that often arises here is how to create a safe, risk-taking, and trusting environment during rehearsals. When I started using rehearsals as a coaching tool, I didn't spend enough time thinking about this. As a result, some teachers shut down when we discussed their rehearsal. Others felt that they were being attacked if someone suggested an alternative teaching move or if we paused instruction to discuss something. As I continued to do this work, I learned some strategies that helped address these very real concerns. Ghousseini et al.'s article "The Fourth Wall of Professional Learning and Cultures of Collaboration" (2022) provided additional guidance for me as I thought about how to support collaboration during rehearsals.

What I found to be helpful in my coaching was similar to what I found to be helpful in my teaching. In both cases, it is really important for me to position myself as a learner and to model being vulnerable. I may be the facilitator, but I am also learning things and often don't have the answer. When I started working with teachers, I often felt this desire to have all the answers or to be the "expert." However, just as with students, I learned that I accomplished a lot when I was authentic and didn't feel the need to always have the right answer. In fact, it was more important to listen to the ways teachers were thinking than to tell them what my feedback was or what I thought the right move was. Increasingly,

I found myself saying, "I don't know. What do you think? Why?" In hindsight, it seems so obvious to listen to teachers' thinking and strategies similar to the way I listen to students' thinking, but it took me some time to make the connection. Once I did, I was able to facilitate learning in a very different way.

This positioning allowed us to have more nuanced conversations about instruction. We could talk about how there is not one right instructional choice. You may make one choice, and I might make another, and neither choice is necessarily wrong or right. Instead, we can look at the affordances and constraints of each option. This sort of discussion can help lay the groundwork for trust.

It's also essential to think about how we position things that don't go as expected, recognizing them as learning opportunities instead of failures. My Favorite Mistake was a tool I often used with students. It enabled me to select a student mistake and highlight how we all learned from it. Similarly, as a coach, I try to frame conversations so that it is expected that we will learn just as much when something goes wrong as we do when it goes right. I get genuinely excited when something happens that we don't expect during a rehearsal or lesson.

As a coach, I highlight the unexpected responses from students for two reasons. First, I really believe we learn from understanding students' responses that we didn't anticipate. Making sense of these new strategies builds our understanding of student thinking. Second, being positive about these unexpected responses takes off the pressure that some teachers put upon themselves to always have everything go exactly the way they want. Knowing that we will learn something that will help our students, whether or not everything goes perfectly, allows us to try new things and take risks without fearing consequences.

Bonus points if I can get admin team members to join in and rehearse as well. Administrators may be worried about losing credibility or authority if they facilitate a routine that doesn't go well, but I've found the opposite outcome happens: teachers respect administrators for taking a chance and working on their teaching craft too.

In addition to setting and supporting norms and creating a risk-taking environment, I also role-play students during rehearsals. My goals are to put forth strategies that are not coming up. For example, I might share a doubling and halving way of solving a problem during a Number Talk if no one else has offered one. That way we can talk about the math and think about how we might respond. Similarly, I might act as a student and share an alternative conception, such as reversing the digits in a subtraction problem because "you can't subtract a bigger number from a smaller one," so that we can discuss how we might address this thinking when it arises (and maybe even discuss the origins of the idea). I plan these moments carefully before the rehearsals. They require me to know my team and what my goals are. For example, if I know that we are working on understanding visual representations, I will strategically try to share out visual strategies so that we can practice representing them.

As seen in the vignette, we sometimes pause the rehearsal to discuss what just happened or determine why we are unsure of what the next move could be. In all cases, after we have completed the rehearsals, we discuss what we learned from them and what our next steps are. The debrief questions I ask as a coach are meant to push thinking and allow us to reflect on what we learned from the experience. Some sample facilitation questions follow. You may want to add ones that are specific to your routine.

FACILITATION QUESTIONS for Rehearsal Debrief

? What did you notice about the student thinking/strategies shared? What questions did the teacher ask to clarify and probe student thinking? To push thinking? What other choices could they have made?

? What happened that we did not anticipate? How did the teacher respond? What other options are there for responding? What are the affordances and constraints of each of these options?

? What choices were made about representing student thinking and making it visible? What other representations might we consider? What are the pros and cons of each of these options?

? What will we change/modify before trying this out with students?

STEP 4 Implement the Routine with Students

After we've had a chance to rehearse the routine with each other, it's time for the teams to try it out with students. We need to consider two things when implementing routines with students. One is whether to try them out with a small group or the whole class. The other thing to think about is whether the teachers will try them with students on their own or whether they will invite others to observe. The choices depend on your goals, the needs of your team, and sometimes logistics and scheduling. Starting with small groups can be less overwhelming for teachers, so at times we start with that. Other times, teachers want to try the routine with the whole class from the beginning to see a range of student responses.

Thinking about whether to have other team members watch is a situation-dependent decision, and you have different options. One idea is to bring in a small group of students during a team meeting so one team member can try out the routine while the rest of the team observes. Other teams might be ready to immediately try out routines with their whole class, with colleagues present, because the team has already built strong relationships and the culture in the school is one where others openly visit classrooms.

You can also think about different ways for the team to gather data. Sometimes team members want to try out the routine on their own a couple times before anyone comes to watch or videotape it. In this case, they can gather artifacts from the lesson, such as student work, pictures of the board, chart-paper recordings, and/or implementation notes, and bring them to the team meeting. If teachers are open to having visitors from the start, the visitors can help record student thinking.

As a coach, your most important move as teachers enact routines is to focus the conversation of the visitors' observations on student thinking: what are students saying and doing? Center the team's feedback on that. I often have the other team member(s) record only what students say or do, while I focus on what the teacher says and does. This structure allows the team member(s) observing to build their skills in understanding student thinking. When we give feedback, the team members focus solely on what students were thinking, while I can strategically highlight questions the teacher asked that opened up student thinking and help us consider what alternate moves we could have made based on student responses.

We can facilitate the debrief of the implementation in different ways. If we are visiting teachers as they implement, the visiting teachers and I sometimes debrief quickly first and then bring in the team member who taught the lesson. Other times, we wait to debrief in a team meeting or PD time after all team members have tried out the routine. And in other cases, we use video and observe and debrief the implementations as a team. However you decide to debrief, the following questions are helpful in guiding the conversation.

FACILITATION QUESTIONS for
Implementation Debrief

? What did you notice about the student thinking/strategies shared? What are some next steps based on their thinking?

? What happened that was similar to when we rehearsed it as a team? What was different?

? What were some similarities and differences about the routines across the different classrooms?

STEP 5 Reflect and Plan Next Steps

After we have implemented the routine with students and debriefed, it is time to think about next steps. As a team, we will decide whether we want to make any modifications to the routine based on the data we gathered from enacting and observing. For example, we might notice that one teacher used sentence stems to provide access to all learners, and we may decide we want to add those during the beginning phase of implementation and then let them fade away naturally as students develop varied, authentic, academic language related to the routine.

We also decide when we want to check in again to discuss how the routine is progressing. I have found that checking in one to two times a month is valuable for keeping the momentum going. It can be helpful to set aside some time during a team meeting to revisit the routine, especially if teachers bring artifacts from their implementations of it. These artifacts could be student work from a Counting Collection or charts from Notice and Wonders. Other times, we will bring in chart paper or a picture of how we recorded thinking from a Number Talk, or we will come with notes we took about strategies that students were using during a Which One Doesn't Belong? activity. Analyzing these artifacts leads to interesting conversations about student thinking and about how we enact the routines.

This phase is also a chance for you as the coach to think about your next steps for both the team and individual team members. For example, some team members might benefit from one-on-one coaching on the routine, which can be the focus of your individual cycles. You also might think about which team members might benefit from observing another team member implement the routine. Or perhaps you see an opportunity for the team to dive deeper into a particular mathematical content area. You might take data on student participation and learning and then work with teachers on ways to make the facilitation of the routines more equitable and accessible. What additional resources or professional development might the team benefit from? Also, how can you work with your admin to ensure that their feedback is in support of and aligns with the new learning from the routine? Taking time to reflect on these questions can help you plan collaborative activities to support the team in their implementation of the routines and plan how you will supplement these team activities with individual coaching cycles.

Rehearsing routines focuses on a small part of lessons and provides a nice starting point for looking at entire lessons. We will investigate lesson study as a way to apply what we've learned to a complete lesson in the next tool.

REFLECTING on LEARNING

- What mathematical routines do your teacher teams currently use? What additional routines might help meet the needs of your team? How will you learn more about the routines that you haven't used personally?

- Once you have decided on a routine, try to complete the planning template in Appendix 5. How will you know whether you met your goals? How will you collect data to formatively assess the team's learning throughout?

- What will be your coaching plan to support the development of the team in implementing the routine? Which team members might need additional one-on-one support? How will you provide it?

EXPLORING the LITERATURE

I first learned about using routines and rehearsals in my work as a teacher educator at the university level. Many teacher educators and researchers have found rehearsals are a useful tool in preparing preservice teachers (Ghousseini 2017; Kazemi and Wæge 2015; Kazemi et al. 2016; Lampert et al. 2013). Rehearsals are meant to mimic the work of teaching and give the teacher educator a chance to provide feedback in the moment.

Kazemi and Wæge (2015) described how the teacher educator plays the following roles during a rehearsal:

1 Providing directive feedback

2 Providing evaluative feedback

3 Scaffolding enactment, for example, by making a teacher move or acting as a student

4 Facilitating a reflective discussion of instructional decisions within the rehearsal

They found that rehearsals allowed the group to work on different parts of teaching and how they relate to one another. When I work with more experienced teachers, I tend to focus on items 3 and 4.

In addition to the work with preservice teachers, there has also been an increased research interest in using rehearsals with teacher teams. Kazemi and Hubbard (2008) looked at the research on professional development and made recommendations for designing and studying PD. One suggestion was to focus on "enactments" of routine instructional activities. They argue that rehearsals of routines provide a common area of focus and allow for multiple enactments during the school year. Rehearsals also allow teachers to dive deeply into questions such as how to use representations or how to respond to student thinking. Researchers have started to study the potential of using rehearsals with in-service teachers across content areas (Kavanagh et al. 2019; Wæge and Fauskanger 2021; Webb and Wilson 2022) and have found them a promising way to develop teachers' practice.

LESSON STUDY
Learning Collectively with Voice, Choice, and Agency

The students in Ms. R's eighth-grade class are working in groups with graph paper, tracing paper, mirrors, and different cut-out shapes. The students are tasked with developing a general rule that could be used to perform different transformations on the coordinate grid, including an argument to justify why their rule will always work.

Four teachers, the assistant principal, and the coach have clipboards in their hands and are circulating and recording what they hear students saying and doing. One teacher snaps photos of student work. The team developed the lesson together in a previous meeting, but today Mr. C is teaching it, even though these are not his regular students. After the lesson, the team gathers around a table to discuss what they saw.

The coach opens the discussion. "Just to remind everyone, we are looking at how we engage middle school students in making sense of mathematics. We want to generalize the findings here so that we can make some recommendations about teaching and learning moving forward. Let's start with Mr. C's thoughts about teaching the lesson we all developed together. To focus us, let's talk about the launch of the task and how it did or didn't engage students in making sense of math. I'll take notes." The group nods. They have previously studied different ways to help students make sense of mathematics on their own.

"Well, I remember that while we were planning, we kept talking about how we would give the students time to just look at the different transformations and write down what they noticed and wondered," Mr. C begins.

"As I said during planning, that seemed like a waste of time. I really thought we should get straight into the task. But it was interesting to hear the connections that they brought to the materials. Even though they couldn't name the transformations or tell us the coordinate rules yet, they were able to easily identify what was happening. Often, I have students who take forever to get started on a task and I need to prompt them repeatedly. But today, the students seemed to all get started right away. Did you all notice that students were able to get right to work at the tables you observed?"

"Yes," Ms. P, a sixth-grade teacher, jumps in. "All the students at the two tables I sat at were jotting things down. One wrote, 'I noticed that sometimes the x-coordinate stays the same and sometimes the y-coordinate stays the same.' I also noted that you gave four minutes of independent think time, which allowed everyone to jot things down, but didn't cause them to go off task."

The coach nods and asks, "Did anyone else write down any observations about the launch?"

A seventh-grade teacher, Ms. S, adds, "My table all started right away. However, some of their noticings and wonderings weren't mathematical. For example, someone wrote, 'I wonder whether this will be on the test next week.'" The group laughs.

The assistant principal jumps in, "I think it's fine if they write things like that down every once in a while. Maybe we could work on helping them refine their noticings as they go on. We could ask them which noticings are helpful in making sense of a problem and which aren't."

Ms. R nods and adds, "I think that one of the bigger ideas I will take away is that Notice and Wonder seemed to give everyone an entry point, and it also allowed us to assess where different students were and what they understood about the coordinate plane."

The coach says, "I'll jot that down under our generalizations. Mr. C, what are you thinking now about the time issue?"

"I think it's something to continue to think about as I plan my own lessons. It seems like the students got started right away. I want to try it and see how it goes in my class," Mr. C responds.

"Great. Let us know how it goes when you try it out. Let's move on to the group task. What strategies did you see students use?"

I've saved lesson study for last because it can be more complex and time intensive than the previous collaborative coaching tools. However, it's also my favorite. Learning about and participating in lesson study was a game-changer for me in terms of thinking about teacher learning and building culture. It changed my perspective on coaching, shifting me from thinking about how I could foster change on my own to how we could learn together.

STOP and JOT

 What did you notice about the previous vignette? What was the coach's role? What learning opportunities were created for the team?

One of the things that stands out to me is that the team is able to talk about the students' thinking and the lesson in a way that allows everyone to be equal participants in the learning. The principal is not observing in an evaluative way; the coach is not modeling a lesson; the teachers are not simply giving feedback to a peer about their lesson. Rather, lesson study provides an opportunity for everyone to think through a lesson together, plan it together, and then analyze and refine teaching and learning together. It allows the team to study a problem they are interested in, take risks, try out new ideas, and then actually see what happens in the classroom, instead of hypothesizing about what will and won't work. In fact, I started doing lesson study because I often heard, "This won't work with my kids," in professional development and team meetings. Lesson study was a way for us, as a team, to engage in hands-on learning. Instead of talking more about the affordances or challenges of some idea, we were able to get in a room and try it out.

Early in my coaching, I made the mistake of modeling whatever strategy or idea teachers were doubtful about. I wanted to say, "See, I told you so. It does work with your kids." Not surprisingly, this can be an unhelpful attitude to have when coaching, and it goes against everything I believe about learning. I wasn't building on what teachers already knew, I wasn't honoring their experience, and I certainly wasn't engaging them in the teaching process. They weren't engaged in all the nuances that go on when we make decisions about planning a lesson or when we make choices in the moment while teaching the lesson. In addition, when I was working in unfamiliar schools, I often didn't know the structures of the classrooms. As a result, classroom management would get in the way, and the strategy or idea would get lost. More importantly, this modeling didn't allow for a systematic way to study a new idea or for productive learning to occur. Finally, trying out lesson study clarified why my one-on-one coaching wasn't successful. I would see tiny incremental changes in individual classrooms, but I wasn't seeing a larger impact that would warrant the time and energy I was spending doing individual coaching. Lesson study seemed to have the potential to create the larger change I was after.

When I started using lesson study, the effect I saw on the teacher teams was incredible. Teachers felt like valuable members of the team, and administrators learned more about the tough choices that go into planning and how complex the work is. We learned from one another, and we learned new things together. Over time, the culture shifted to one where teachers asked to do a lesson study when they were struggling with a problem of practice. I would hear things like, "I don't know how to implement parts of this new curriculum. Can we do a lesson study to think about these exploration centers they talk about?" or "I want to explore how to do more problem-based lessons with my students, but it's not working when I try it on my own. Can we do a lesson study?" or "I want to explore how to build on the strengths of my multilingual students. Can we do a lesson study?" Lesson study becomes such a part of the culture that when we are faced with a problem, the team may not be able to solve it, but we can learn more about it through lesson study.

And that's the main reason I think lesson study works: *it is a vehicle for studying problems of practice collaboratively.* Teachers come across problems and questions about teaching and learning all the time. All too often, they are left on their own to solve these problems. Sure, they have informal conversations about them with their colleagues and are given feedback during observations, but schools rarely provide them with the tools and support they need to examine the problems they are most interested in studying. Lesson study creates a risk-free way to explore problems and experiment with solutions to address these problems.

Lesson study also becomes a learning opportunity for administrators. They often know what they want to see in a classroom but are unclear why they are not seeing it. Participating in the lesson study process helps administrators see inside the heads of their teams as they plan and offers them insight into the decisions that are being made. In addition, the administrators bring a different perspective to the group, and together we all learn more about teaching and learning math.

All that said, lesson study can be time-consuming. Although I've tried to keep the integral parts of lesson study as described in the literature, I've had to adapt some of the systems and structures to make it work in schools and be a realistic part of the culture and professional learning. I've also been inspired by the creative work on Learning Labs and Math Labs (Kazemi et al. 2018). After about five years of tinkering together, my colleagues in one school and I have adapted Math Labs and lesson study to make a PD structure that works well for collaborative coaching, which I'll share later. You may find that you need to modify even further to meet the needs of your teams.

LESSON STUDY AS A COACHING TOOL

Lesson study was developed in Japan as a systematic way for groups of teachers to study their practice together (Takahashi and McDougal 2016). Lesson study teams choose a research focus (e.g., differentiation, lesson synthesis, questioning) and then study different ways to address this area of interest. Next, the team collaboratively plans a lesson incorporating what they've learned, and then one member of the team implements the lesson, with the rest of the team observing and collecting different information. After the lesson is taught, the team analyzes the lesson and makes generalizations about what they have learned about teaching and learning. The process of debriefing the lesson often leads to new research questions, and the cycle begins again (see Figure 6.1).

The entire process focuses on examining student thinking through these "study

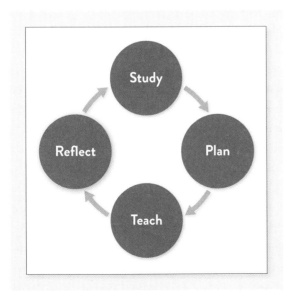

Figure 6.1 The lesson study cycle

lessons." Catherine Lewis, who has done a lot of work on lesson study in the United States, explained how lesson studies often move the focus of the work to the students: "Japanese teachers often mentioned as a major benefit of lesson study 'the eyes to see children (kodomo wo miru me)'" (Lewis 2002, 13). Shifting our focus from examining the teacher and the teaching to looking at the learning and the learner has been a theme for all the coaching I do, but it's especially important in lesson study. The lesson we create is an opportunity for us all to work together and use our collective experience and knowledge to think about instruction. Our analysis of the lesson allows us to refine what we know about how best to foster students' thinking. Lesson study is not about creating one perfect lesson but, rather, it's about using this one lesson as a "case of" something larger—a chance for us to learn together about a particular aspect of teaching and learning.

I have to confess that I have never been to Japan and seen lesson study as it is done there. I have had the opportunity to visit a Japanese school here in the United States, The Japanese School of New York, and was able to witness how they do lesson study. I've also read a lot about the process, and I'm pretty sure that what I have been doing is a modification of Japanese lesson study. I like to think that the versions we have created in our schools stick true to the main principles but are adapted for our contexts. Sometimes I say that the process we use is "lesson study–inspired," and it's the outgrowth of many years of collaboration and experimentation with my partnering schools.

When I was first ready to try lesson study, I was lucky to work with administrators in a K–8 school who embraced and supported the idea. The admin team was committed to developing inquiry-based classrooms and had a vision of what they might look like, but none of them were experts in teaching math. We decided to start with the middle-school math team. The team included experienced math teachers with strong content knowledge. However, there was still a bit of resistance about moving to a more conceptual, student-centered way of teaching. Lesson study became a way for us all to learn how to develop a more inquiry-based way of teaching math. Together, we created structures and systems that made lesson study part of the school's culture. Eventually we moved lesson study to the K–5 classrooms and even to other subject areas. Over the past five years, we've conducted countless lesson studies and made modifications to the process that helped make it a sustainable initiative for the school. We have also learned much together as a team. I often hear the administrators in the building talking about the mathematics in a way that is so much more nuanced than when we started. In addition, the teachers are far more willing to experiment and take risks than they were at the start of the work. And although my faith in test scores is not very high, others seem to find it compelling that the scores in the building rose over these years.

We continue to experiment with our lesson study model, inspired by Elham Kazemi and her colleagues' work on Math Labs (Kazemi et al. 2018). In Math Labs, small teams of teachers coplan a lesson, implement it together, and then debrief the lesson, which allows teachers to experiment with their instruction collaboratively. Two differences between Math Labs and lesson study are that, in Math Labs, (1) the teachers enact the lesson *together*, and (2) teachers discuss instructional decisions *in the moment*, as well as during planning and debriefing. The work is led by a teacher educator and allows for teachers to experiment with their instruction collaboratively. When I learned about Math Labs, I was intrigued by these ideas of teachers making instructional decisions together and teaching together during the lesson. Sometimes, I have teachers do this during lesson study, but I normally launch lesson study with one person leading the lesson and the other participants observing student thinking. Later on, we sometimes move toward making decisions together during the lesson.

I have included resources at the end of the section for you to learn more about lesson study and Math Labs. You'll find great work to build on, and it's important to read and learn and think as much about these approaches as possible before starting out with a group. Then you'll be able to decide which modifications work for you.

LESSON STUDY IN ACTION

As the coach, you play an important role in all aspects of the cycle shown in Figure 6.1, including helping teachers choose a research question that they want to study, providing resources to help them learn more about their research topic, creating tools and structures for all aspects of the process (planning, implementing, and debriefing the lesson), and helping the team to make generalizations about the learning. You'll also maintain focus on building trust and community within the group. Lesson study has the potential to lose momentum, to be started and then abandoned because of the time commitment and the amount of work required. For it to be sustainable, structures have to be in place so that lesson study is systematic and manageable. For me, the following steps have been helpful in implementing lesson study.

STEP 1 Develop a research question

STEP 2 Research our question

STEP 3 Plan and rehearse

STEP 4 Implement

STEP 5 Debrief

STEP 6 Summarize and share

As you read through the specifics of each step, you may find the Lesson Study Planning Template to be helpful, which you can find in Appendix 6a and on the 6 Tools website. I like to use it to sketch out my learning plan for the team before I begin the work. As with any lesson plan with students, you can modify and adjust as you move along in the process, but it allows me to be clear about my goals and plan at the start of the work.

STEP 1 Develop a Research Question

An important part of lesson study is that it is not about creating a perfect lesson but, rather, about using the lesson to learn something about teaching and learning, and this learning begins with a question. We often ask questions such as, "How can I help my students develop a better understanding of fractions?" or "How am I going to use these curriculum materials with my students?" or "How can I facilitate a mathematical conversation that engages all learners?" Learning to study questions in a systematic way is what lesson study is for.

Research questions often come out of learning walks or team meetings. As coaches, we can look for opportunities that arise when teams are struggling with a particular problem of practice and then offer up those questions as suggestions for lesson study. We can also have teachers brainstorm the things that they want to learn more about. Some facilitation questions follow that may help the team select a research question. You may want to add your own as well.

FACILITATION QUESTIONS for Selecting a Research Question

- **?** What are some strategies we want to learn more about?
- **?** What are some content areas we want to learn more about?
- **?** What are some practices we want to use to better support our students?

Using these or other prompts as a launching point, you'll want to facilitate the conversation so that the entire team has input into the research question. Often, the team comes to consensus about the question fairly easily. Other times, I try to facilitate the conversation by highlighting a topic that the team is curious about. Sometimes that curiosity comes in the form of excitement about a new idea, and other times, it presents in the form of skepticism. Many of the most interesting lesson studies I have been part of have resulted from us exploring a strategy or idea where some (or all) members were convinced it wouldn't be successful. Testing out our hypothesis is part of the process, and not knowing what will happen gives us a chance to learn. If we already know exactly what is going to happen, we don't need to engage in lesson study. The interesting learning happens when we explore the unexpected.

Here are some research questions teams have used. I share them as examples of the work we have done, but remember that the beauty of lesson study is that the team and the context shape what is studied based on what is meaningful and relevant to them, so resist the urge to pick one of these without engaging in that process.

Curriculum: How can we modify, improve, or adapt a particular program or strategy the district has chosen to meet the needs of our students?

Discussions: How do we foster a productive classroom discussion?

Productive partnerships: How do we help students work productively in groups or partners?

Centers: How might we use centers to help differentiate content for our students?

Engagement: How do we engage students in content so that it is meaningful and relevant to their lives?

Equity and Access: How do we best incorporate culturally sustaining pedagogies into our classrooms?

Mathematical Practices: How do we help students develop a mathematical argument?

Content Areas: How do we help students develop a conceptual understanding of fractions, algebra, addition, and so on?

Manipulatives: How can concrete objects be used to help students foster understanding of a particular content area?

Coteaching: How can the special education and content teachers work together to best support students in a math classroom?

After we have crafted the research question, we come up with some hypotheses so we can develop concrete strategies that may help answer our question. For example, if we are trying to develop students' ability to problem solve and make sense of fractions, we may have a hunch that tasks need multiple entry points and that manipulatives need to be available so students can touch and see fractional quantities. This hunch gives us a place to start our research in step 2 (is our hunch supported by research?) and allows us to focus our lesson planning (step 3) on whatever strategy we want to test out.

Another thing to think about is the makeup of the lesson study teams. Will the teams be mixed-grade levels or same-grade level? Will special education teachers and multilingual teachers be included? Will paraprofessionals be included? These questions don't have any right answers: the goals of the work determine who will be on the teams. For example, sometimes it is helpful to have a grade-level team look at a particular discussion strategy and then share what they learned with other grades. Other times, it is helpful to have different-grade team members look at a content area—say, fractions—so that there is some understanding of the conceptual development of the content across grade levels. I also find it incredibly important to have an administrator on the team who is an active participant and who positions themselves as a learner.

STEP 2 Research Our Question

Once we've picked our topic, it's important to think about how we will build on the existing resources that are related to the topic. The Japanese call this *kyouzai kenkyuu* (Takahashi and Yoshida 2004). It is a chance for teachers to explore some of the resources that currently exist surrounding the content and teaching strategies related to their research question. It's also a chance for them to revise their hypothesis based on what they find. This process reminds me of a literature review that researchers do before beginning a study. The goal is to build on the work of others and not have to start from scratch.

Researching is one of my favorite parts of lesson study. I love having the time to explore the mathematics of the lesson and the different approaches that have been developed for fostering students' understanding of the content. It's also the step where I try to do the groundwork for the team. I usually make sure we have different curriculum resources, manipulatives, research articles, and other materials available. Teachers are encouraged to bring their own research as well, but taking the literature dive off their plate and allowing myself, as the coach, time to become an expert in what is out there can really help the learning of the team and can help the process be more efficient and manageable.

Let's think back to the fraction question I posed in step 1: "How can I help my students develop a better understanding of fractions?" During step 2, I would gather all the fractions manipulatives I could find, make available a trajectory of fraction development, pull some research articles about fractions, and see how the particular objective we are teaching (let's say, introducing fractions) is handled across several different curricula. Then during the team meeting or PD time, we would break off into pairs, examine the different materials, and discuss what we learned. After these partner conversations, we would discuss what strategies or ideas we want to test out in our lesson. Sometimes, these discussions lead to refinement of the research question. For example, we may decide we want to narrow our focus to the manipulatives we will use to introduce fractions, so our question might be changed to "What fraction models can be used at the start of a fraction unit to help students develop a better understanding of fractions?" Once we have summarized what we have learned and decided what we want to test out in our lesson study, we can move onto the specifics of the lesson planning.

STEP 3 Plan and Rehearse

The planning time is very much informed by the research we did on our topic. In fact, we usually have a general idea and outline of the plan after reviewing the materials, so we can now discuss the specifics of the lesson and try to anticipate different strategies and ideas students might bring to the task. The host teacher will use this time to give specific information about students, help us think about strategic grouping, and discuss the current routines and structures that exist in their classroom. They can provide the team with context and data, which helps the team tailor the lesson to the students that we will be teaching.

The lesson plan used for lesson study is generally much more detailed than an everyday lesson plan. (I've included a sample template that I have used with teams in Appendix 6b and on the 6 Tools website, but it is a flexible tool, and you may want to modify it based on your context.) We often script parts out and include details about specific strategies we plan on trying. The idea is not that you would plan every lesson to this level of detail, but rather that this amount of planning allows us to be precise about what it is we are studying. Sometimes a teacher will say to me, "Well, of course, if we had this much time to plan and had five people on the team to help us, our lessons would be different." When I hear that, I realize that we are missing the point of lesson study and that I need to go back and reframe the conversation and remind the team that this is a lesson that will be used to study something about teaching and learning and not a "model" lesson plan.

As the coach, I often do the actual writing of the lesson plan during step 3. This scribing allows me to ask clarifying questions, probe thinking, and focus the conversation so that specifics are included in the lesson plan. I generally create the document in a way that everyone sees what I am writing while we are planning—perhaps via a shared Google Doc or by projecting my screen on a SMART Board.

After we have planned the lesson together, we decide who will teach the lesson. Because it is a shared lesson, anyone in the group can teach it. Think about your goals for the team and the individual members on it when determining who will teach the lesson. Often we decide as a team, but sometimes I strongly encourage a particular team member to teach it based on our goals. I often push administrators to teach at least one of the lessons so that we can all be equal participants in the process. Sometimes I teach the lessons, sometimes the teacher in whose classroom we are implementing the lesson teaches the lesson, and sometimes a different team member leads the lesson. Each of these options offers affordances and constraints. For example, when I teach the lesson, it can have an unintended effect of coming off as a model lesson. I have to be really strategic in setting the expectation that we are looking at the lesson we all created. Having administrators teach the lesson puts them in a vulnerable position. This can be great for positioning them as learners along with the team but can also be problematic if the team doesn't yet trust them. Knowing your team members, you can make the choice that best meets the team's needs.

After the lesson is typed up, everyone reviews and revises it once more. If we have time, we sometimes rehearse it with the team acting as students. This step can be valuable because it allows us to practice and anticipate different things that might happen during the lesson. However, sometimes we skip this step due to time. It's up to you whether you think that the team would benefit from this rehearsal and whether your schedules allow for it.

We also use the planning time for another important task—deciding what data to collect during the lesson, who will collect which data, and how we will gather it. We try to tie this collection of data directly to the research goal. For example, if our goal is to look at how students are making sense of problems, then we might track how many students get started on the task without prompting, what students are struggling with, what questions seem to help students get started, what materials students reach for, and/or how much wait time they are given.

As we plan what data to collect, we also decide which team members will observe and record different aspects of the lesson or different aspects of the classroom so we gather all the data we possibly can. I also strategically select what I am responsible for observing, as opposed to the rest of the team. For example, I may have the team focus on observing students, while I record the teachers' questions. This move allows me to make sure I highlight certain aspects related to questioning, while keeping the team's focus on the students.

This is also a good time to discuss how data will be collected. Will we use a template? Will we use time stamps? Is someone tracking participation? Is a simple T-chart sufficient, or do we need something more complex? One note-taker example is provided in Appendix 6c and on the 6 Tools website, but it might be helpful for the team to modify this template based on their goals.

Before we implement the lesson, I usually ensure all resources for the lesson are gathered, the lesson plans are shared with all members of the team, and the note-taking forms are available. Now it's time to implement the lesson that we have worked so hard on!

STEP 4 Implement

The biggest challenge with implementation is often scheduling. It can be difficult to free up teachers to allow them to attend the lesson. Talking with the administration about the logistics and reiterating the importance of having everyone present is a key part of our role as coaches. If at least one administrator is on board, they can figure out a way to cover teachers during the lesson. A benefit of including an administrator as part of the team is they see firsthand the value of lesson study and are more likely to support logistics for future lesson studies.

Once you have a time on the calendar and the team freed up to watch the lesson, you can make sure the teacher teaching the lesson feels prepared and has all the supplies ready. You can also meet with the observing teachers for a quick recap of what data they are collecting and ensure they have their note-takers and a copy of the lesson plan. As we move forward in lesson study, we will often use teacher time-outs to discuss teaching moves we aren't sure of as a team, but in the first few lesson studies, it can be helpful for everyone to observe.

One issue that often comes up during the lesson is that the observers have a difficult time not helping students. They want to assist when a student is struggling or has a question and help them work through the problem or ask them guiding questions. Just before the lesson, remind the team that they are collecting data that will ultimately help students, but at the moment, it is important not to help students who may have their hands raised.

I encourage everyone to take snapshots of student work as they are observing because interesting things happen while students solve problems. At the end of the lesson, we collect all student work. I also capture what the teacher has written on the board with a camera. These photos are particularly helpful when we are looking at representations. The more data we collect, the richer our debrief conversation and analysis will be. Table 6.1 summarizes the different roles of the team members and may be helpful as you plan your implementation.

STEP 5 Debrief

Traditional lesson study has a strict protocol for conducting the debrief. However, I've adapted it to meet the needs of our schools. The most important aspect is to keep the conversation focused on the research goal and purpose of the lesson study. We want to look at the specifics of the lesson and examine the student work, while thinking about what this particular lesson shows us about teaching and learning more generally. Our goal is not to refine this one lesson, as is the case in traditional lesson study, but rather to think about what we might address in our teaching overall. For example, what implications does this eighth-grade algebra lesson have for a first-grade teacher? What about teaching and learning did we learn that is new or that surprised us?

When I facilitate the debrief, I also take notes and capture what the group is saying, and I position myself as a learner throughout. I focus us first on analyzing the lesson we observed, and then I move the team to generalizing what we learned that could be applied to our teaching. I focus on the lesson and not on

Table 6.1

Different roles of the team members during lesson study implementation

ADMINISTRATION	COACH	TEACHER
Create and schedule opportunity for the team to participate in and observe the lesson.	Actively participate in the implementation, either teaching the lesson or observing.	Actively participate in the implementation, either teaching the lesson or observing.
Actively participate in the implementation, either teaching the lesson or observing.	Set the tone for the observing teachers, reminding them of norms.	Observation norms: • Take low-inference notes. • Listen to student thinking and record it.
Set the tone for the observing teachers, reminding them of norms.	If the lesson is taught twice, conduct a quick debrief with the team in between.	• Monitor student progress, paying close attention to checks for understanding. • Do not help students or answer student questions—direct to the teacher, if needed.

the teacher who taught the lesson. This framing highlights students' thinking and also makes the debrief more productive.

We usually start by asking the person who taught the lesson to share their point of view, and then we share evidence we found. I push the group to support any claims they make with evidence. We then examine student work from the lesson to see what additional information that imparts. Throughout the process, I push for us to make generalizations about teaching and learning when it is appropriate. In many ways, facilitating the debrief is similar to facilitating a classroom conversation, because we are using questions to guide the group to come to some conclusions. In the classroom, we draw conclusions about mathematical ideas, and in lesson study, we draw conclusions about teaching and learning. I am constantly surprised by what we learn during lesson study and how ideas that I never would have thought of are brought to the table. It's the power of the team looking at a lesson together that brings this new learning.

The final step of the debrief is to refine our research goal and decide on next steps based on what we learned. Then we can begin the cycle again.

STEP 6 Summarize and Share

After the debrief is completed, I like to create a record of what we learned. These notes allow others who may not have participated to read about what we learned, allow us to share with new team members, and, finally, help us hang on to the learning. When I first started coaching, I kept records of work I did with individual teachers, but I wasn't great at creating shared records of what we learned as a team. When we share our findings, we specify what we learned. Our cumulative record also allows us to keep track of what we learned year to year or month to month.

As the coach, I write the first draft of the findings we discussed in the debrief, which takes a burden off teachers, who already have enough on their plates. I then share my draft and remind everyone that it is a group document so that all the team members can make changes. Figure 6.2 shows a document that I created after an initial lesson study with an eighth-grade team who wanted to investigate a recently adopted, inquiry-based curriculum. In our initial meetings, we discussed the need for modifications of the materials to improve accessibility while maintaining focus on the department's goal that students make sense of problems and persevere. The team came up with the following research question: *How can we modify our curricular materials to engage students in problem solving and increase perseverance?* We read some articles such as "Three Strategies for Opening Curriculum Spaces" (Drake et al. 2015) and examined the lesson plans in the curriculum. After investigating the resources, we decided to try rearranging the lesson components and planned and implemented a lesson that frontloaded problem solving and gave students time to explore the task at the start of the lesson. I summarized our debrief conversation and shared my notes with the team for their input before sending it out to the entire math team at the school.

One thing you might notice is that the evidence from the low-inference observation notes isn't included in the summary. This team had done several rounds of lesson study, so we had a shared understanding of what evidence was used to make statements. However, when you start with lesson study, you may want to include examples from the note-taking sheets, such as students' quotes, to help give examples and support for these claims. You will also see that we include not only what we learned about the research question but also what we learned about lesson study. This reflection allows us to continue refining our process.

DATES: 11/21 (Planning) 11/24 (Implementation)	TEAM MEMBERS: Ms. H, Mr. L, Ms. G, Ms. R

RESEARCH QUESTION: How can we modify our curricular materials to engage students in problem solving and increase perseverance?

WHAT WE LEARNED ABOUT . . .

Our Modification of the Curriculum Materials

- The <u>video</u> was engaging for students. It made a real-world connection between computer animation and transformations. This hooked the eighth graders into the lesson.
- As we noticed with sixth graders in our prior lesson study, <u>partner work</u> (as opposed to groups of four) made it easier to hold students accountable.
- A <u>monitoring sheet</u> helped the teacher circulate and record the strategies students used. It also helped the teacher determine which strategies could be shared with the whole class and in what order.
- We needed to <u>modify</u> the shape that students were given in Part B so that it had fewer points for them to translate. Even with this modification, the problem was still difficult. Our debrief between lessons allowed us to brainstorm a strategy that helped make Part B more accessible: drawing the arrows on the figures in Part A so it could be connected to Part B.
- We noticed <u>vocabulary</u> was an obstacle for some students. During the debrief, it was suggested that there be a place in the room to record important words the teacher hears as students share out or are exploring in groups.
- Similar to what we noticed in sixth grade, <u>charting</u> out the key ideas of the class discussion focused students on the main points and connected to the learning target.
- Students worked at their own <u>pace</u>. There were bonus activities for those who finished early. Students were not pressured to finish every problem but rather encouraged to focus on the important ones that the teacher highlighted.

Creating Problem Solvers/Increasing Perseverance

- The exploration phase of the lesson was challenging: many students didn't know how to get started, were off-task, and so forth. Successful teacher interventions included asking students to <u>make a prediction</u> where a point might be, asking <u>whether an answer made sense</u>, showing students an <u>alternate solution</u> and asking why someone may have got that solution, and asking students <u>how they could check</u> whether they were right.
- Knowing when to allow students to struggle and when to jump in with a hint are important decisions to make. One possible intervention that was discussed was to create <u>hint sheets</u> that kids can access when they are stuck.

(continued)

Figure 6.2 Example lesson study summary

Lesson Study

- This was a great lesson for lesson study because it was difficult for students, so we were able to watch what happens when they struggle. Posing a more challenging task was easier to do as a group than it might have been individually because we were able to brainstorm together how to support students on the task.

- Unlike in sixth grade, this was not an introduction lesson, so we were able to see a different type of lesson.

- Planning is so important. We scribbled all over our teacher's guides while doing the problems and made lots of notes. We also brainstormed ways to make the text more accessible without removing the rigor.

- We still need more time to debrief between the lessons so that we can make modifications for the next class.

- It was nice for teachers to be able to listen to students talking about the problem and how they were thinking without feeling pressure to jump in and help them.

- Reflecting on a lesson is something many of us often do in isolation. It was noted that it was nice to reflect with others.

Figure 6.2 Example lesson study summary (continued)

STOP and JOT

 What do you notice about what was summarized? What might you do differently?

THE OUTCOME: LEARNING COLLECTIVELY WITH VOICE, CHOICE, AND AGENCY

One of the concerns you might have about lesson study is the investment it requires. Teachers need to be freed up, schedules need to be adjusted, and coverage or sub money needs to be allocated toward it. These are all serious challenges. However, the response I've received from teacher teams makes me certain it is worth the investment. Here are some quotes from teachers who have participated in lesson study with me:

"Lesson study has allowed me to rethink traditional teaching strategies. Things that I thought 'must work' or 'won't work' are now being called into question."

"After seeing the impact of real student-centered learning activities on student understanding, I have tried to create more of these opportunities for my students."

"This is the most interactive PD I have ever been a part of. It is directly linked to our department and school goals. We can be told a million times how we should plan and deliver lessons, but if we are not given an opportunity to practice and implement them with guidance, we are usually unable to do these things on our own."

"I try now to facilitate questioning more instead of direct teaching. I thought this professional development was more beneficial than others in the past because I was an active participant."

"We are able to work with our colleagues, coach, and administration to plan a lesson. Having admin involved was so beneficial these few years because it allowed for a real partnership to form during our planning sessions."

STOP and JOT

What do you notice about these responses? What about using lesson study as a tool allows for these types of responses?

What I hear in these responses is that teachers appreciate being actively involved and being given the opportunity to practice. When I think about coaching, I often think about what opportunities I give the team to practice new skills. Lesson study is one way to provide practice. It gives us the time to learn more about teaching and learning and then gives us a safe space to practice what we've learned. The first quote (*"Lesson study has allowed me to rethink traditional teaching strategies. Things that I thought 'must work' or 'won't work' are now being called into question."*) speaks to me the most because it points to an important belief I hold as a coach—that learning often involves unlearning. The more opportunities I can create for us to question things that we have always believed to be true, the more we can learn together.

As I said earlier, lesson study purists will probably have many concerns about the ways in which I describe the process here. However, these modifications are how I have made the process work for my schools. I hope that you will be inspired to make it work for you.

REFLECTING on LEARNING

- What are some questions about teaching and learning that have come up in your work that might make for good lesson study research questions?

- How might you adapt lesson study for your context?

- What challenges do you anticipate? How might you address them?

- How can you use lesson study along with other tools in your work?

EXPLORING the LITERATURE

As I mentioned earlier, lesson study originated in Japan and has been an important feature of professional learning in schools there. Researchers have found that lesson study has been helpful in improving Japanese elementary school teachers' teaching (Lewis and Tsuchida 1998; Stigler and Hiebert 2009; Takahashi 2000; Yoshida 1999).

Lesson study first became popular in the United States in 2009 when the book *The Teaching Gap* was published by Stigler and Hiebert. The authors included a chapter on lesson study in Japan and called for U.S. educators to try lesson study in their schools. Since then, many districts have tried using lesson study and researchers have examined the implementation. The Lesson Study Group at Mills College (www.lessonresearch.net) has done a great deal of work on the topic. Of particular interest from their work is a randomized, controlled study done by Lewis and Perry (2014) that showed a significant impact of lesson study on teachers' knowledge. Rebecca R. Perry and Catherine C. Lewis also presented a successful case of a district adapting lesson study in the United States in "What Is Successful Adaptation of Lesson Study in the U.S.?" (2009). In addition to detailing the successes of implementing lesson study, the authors also discuss the challenges in implementing lesson study, and they emphasize that the changes took time. These findings can be helpful to remember as you begin lesson study in your schools.

Another group of researchers who discuss how to adapt lesson study in the United States are Akihiko Takahashi and Thomas McDougal. Their article "Collaborative Lesson Research: Maximizing the Impact of Lesson Study" (2016) details what they learned from studying five schools that used lesson study. Based on these case studies, they identified the following four key factors that are important for lesson study to be successful:

- The school leader is enthusiastic about lesson study, and the faculty is aware of this enthusiasm.
- In addition to the school leader, another lesson study advocate is part of the faculty.
- A schoolwide goal for teaching and learning exists and is compelling.
- The school administration is committed to provide time and support for lesson study.

As the coach, you can get an administrator on board and be the other advocate in the building.

In addition to the lesson study research, the work on Math Labs may also be of interest to you. As I mentioned earlier, Math Labs are similar in many ways to lesson studies. Math Labs include four stages: learning, coplanning a lesson, implementing the lesson together, and debriefing (McDonald, Kazemi, and Kavanagh 2013). A main difference is that the team both plans and implements the lesson together. During the lesson, the team will discuss instructional decisions in the moment. In addition, the lessons are also more exploratory in nature than lesson study. In one case study of a coach who implemented Math Labs with a fourth-grade team, the researchers found that the coach was able to support collective inquiry and learning using Math Labs (Gibbons et al. 2017).

Teachers came to a mutual understanding of high-quality instructional practice and further refined their skills. If you want to know more about Math Labs, a great article to take a look at is "Math Labs: Teachers, Teacher Educators, and School Leaders Learning Together with and from Their Own Students" (Kazemi et al. 2018). You may also want to listen to this podcast: https://amplify .com/math-teacher-lounge/episode-s3-03/, which is linked on the 6 Tools website.

Finally, some additional resources that may be useful to you as you begin your work on lesson study are the following two books:

- *Lesson Study Step by Step: How Teacher Learning Communities Improve Instruction* (2011).

- *Leading Lesson Study: A Practical Guide for Teachers and Facilitators* (2006).

The Lesson Study Group at Mills College also has some excellent videos of the different stages of lesson study, which are linked on the 6 Tools website.

REFLECTING AND GROWING

Let's say you've built community and you tried out one (or more) of the tools mentioned in the book so far. Now what? For me, coaching is a constant cycle of reflecting and learning and modifying. I try out a new strategy or tool, I reflect on what worked, I think about what I learned from the experience, I adapt and modify my plan, and then I repeat the cycle. This process of reflecting and refining my plans is what keeps the work interesting for me.

I find it helpful to reflect on the work in both the short term and the long term. For example, I might reflect on how a particular tool, like lesson study, is working after I implement it and then plan for my next steps for the teams. I also take time to reflect on how things are going in the longer term, perhaps at the end of a school year, to think about the impact of the coaching overall and how to improve my work. Let's start with how I reflect after I've implemented a specific tool.

Coaching cycle

REFLECTING ON THE SHORT-TERM IMPACTS OF A COACHING TOOL

After planning and implementing a tool—say, rehearsing routines—I take some time to reflect on how the strategy worked. I look carefully at any data I've collected, such as student work, team meeting notes, classroom visit notes and pictures, and my notes from the team's debrief meetings. I reflect on what worked and what didn't. I often start with examining how well the team members collaborated. Were they willing to take risks? Were they receptive to feedback from one another? Or was there some resistance? Sometimes we need to go back to the community-building activities in Tool 1 if the team is having trouble working together.

I also consider what my goals were for using the tool and whether we met them. For example, if the goal was to do a lesson study that allowed the team to explore discourse in classrooms, did we come up with some strategies for increasing classroom discussion? Am I seeing these strategies when I visit classrooms for individual coaching sessions? Depending on the answers to these questions, I then think about what our next steps should be and how to modify the plan. Should we do another lesson study? Should we modify our research question or look at more resources on discussion? Or do we want to rehearse specific routines that might help the team develop their classroom discussion moves? Once I decide on the modification, I start planning how we will either modify the tool or choose a new one, and the cycle begins again.

REFLECTING ON THE LONG-TERM IMPACTS OF COACHING

In addition to reflecting on how a specific tool is working, it can be helpful to reflect on your long-term coaching. How do you know whether your coaching is working? I often do this type of reflection at the end of the school year, thinking about the impact the work is having on teacher teams, students, and other stakeholders. I use a similar cycle to the previous one, but instead of focusing on a specific tool, I consider my overall coaching work for the year. What was my plan at the beginning of my work with the team? Did I meet my goals for the team? I reflect on the different tools I implemented and collect data on the impact of the coaching. After I review what the team has learned, I think about what modifications I can make to my overall coaching work. I use these ideas to create a plan for the following year. Even if I'm not working with the school again, I have found this process helpful in improving my skills as a coach so that I can apply what I have learned to other schools or districts.

REFLECTING ON THE IMPACT ON DIFFERENT GROUPS

Whether I am reflecting on the short-term or long-term impacts of my coaching work, the following three questions help guide my reflection process:

- How is the coaching impacting teacher teams?
- How is the coaching impacting students?
- How is the coaching impacting other stakeholders?

In the following sections, we will dive deeper into each question.

How Is the Coaching Impacting Teacher Teams?

One way to determine whether our coaching is effective is to analyze the feedback we receive from teachers. It's important to reflect on both solicited and unsolicited feedback. When I began coaching, teachers' reflections and emails sounded like the following representative examples:

"Nicora, thanks again for talking with me about Number Talks and showing me how one looks in my class. I think that I'm going to try out Number Talks again in the class. I'll keep you updated on how they go."

"I'm thinking about what we discussed about wait time. I'm going to try to count to three more often in my head. I think it will help give students some more time to process the problem."

Part of me felt good about this feedback because teachers were using the new strategies we talked about. I was happy to hear that an aspect of their practice was changing right away, and I knew that small changes in practice often start a domino effect that leads to bigger changes. Another part of me, however, felt that I could be doing more. I wanted to create a culture of learning and curiosity that was sustainable and that was driven by the teacher teams. Sometimes I still felt like the teacher at the front of the board, directing the learning. Teachers were waiting for me to share a strategy and then they would implement it. I also wondered whether I had developed a procedural understanding of strategies among the teachers but not the conceptual understanding of *why* we were using these strategies. For example, teachers might be following the procedures of Number Talks correctly, but they weren't using the routine as a tool to uncover student thinking because they didn't understand the rationale behind the routine. Teachers mechanically implementing routines reminded me of students following the algorithm for subtraction without really understanding regrouping. They might know the steps of certain student-centered strategies, like Number Talks, but they hadn't deeply learned *how or why* we do them.

After I shifted to using more collaborative coaching tools that focused on student thinking, the feedback I received from teachers shifted, too. The text messages you see are from a seventh-grade teacher. We had been working on moving from the concrete to the abstract with students. The seventh-grade teacher was visiting the sixth-grade teacher's class and sent me these animated texts right from the classroom.

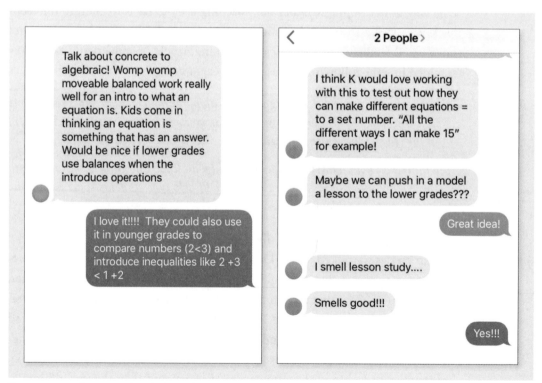

Text messages from a teacher during a classroom visit

Now we were looking at problems of practice together and thinking about the tools that might help us solve them, such as lesson study. This shift reminded me of when my students began asking the questions and I provided the tools to help them. Similarly, the teacher teams were directing their learning. I still provided the structures and the systems, but they were leading the inquiry.

I also started receiving messages that focused on student thinking. Instead of requests that read, "Do you have any activities for teaching proportion?" I started receiving photographs of student work with messages from teachers who wanted to analyze student thinking together. These types of messages make me smile because curiosity about student thinking is the gateway to shifting our practice. When our lens moves from teachers' moves to students' thinking, we see and learn new and different things. Instead of looking for a lesson plan or a curriculum that will solve all our problems, we begin to look at students' thinking and build our approach from there. We see our students differently, and we see our practice differently. I feel most successful as a teacher and a coach when I foster a new way of looking at the world. I feel this way when I'm not the only one in the room excited to share what I heard a student say or to grapple with the hard questions about why a student is thinking a certain way. When teachers become curious, that's an indicator that we are successfully shifting how we view our students and our work.

We can notice impact in other ways as well. You may notice shifts in department or whole-school faculty meetings. Teachers might share artifacts from their classrooms that reflect the shifts they are seeing in their teaching and in students' learning. For example, one math department started adjusting the way they used talk moves to increase math conversation. During a whole-school faculty meeting, the topic of classroom conversation came up, and teachers shared the strategies they were trying out and the growth they'd

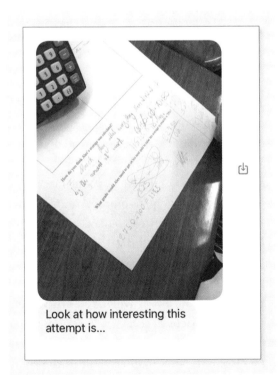

Look at how interesting this attempt is...

A text message from a teacher about student work

observed in the level of students' discussions. Paying attention to this spontaneous sharing and enthusiasm about the work is another way to notice impact.

How Is the Coaching Impacting Students?

Another question that guides my work is: *what's the impact on our students?* There are many ways to look at this question. For example, when I started to use more collaborative tools with teachers, I began to notice changes when I visited their classrooms. Students had more opportunities to make sense of problems, and teachers were listening to students share strategies. I noticed students were more engaged when teachers were trying strategies they had rehearsed with the teams or when teachers used ideas they learned from lesson study.

I know that another way that we measure success is through student test scores. I have my doubts about using test scores to measure achievement, but I will share some of these results as another data point. I started working with an urban K–8 school with individual coaching. In year two, we moved toward a more collaborative coaching model, and we have made gains over the years since then.

	Year One	Year Two	Year Three	Year four	Year five
Math proficiency	35%	36%	41%	51%	58%

I share these scores because I know that so many of our schools and teachers are under immense pressure to meet certain scores. And I'd be lying if I didn't admit that seeing these gains gave me credibility with certain people who weren't convinced by other measures that mean more to me.

I also look for changes in students' attitudes and beliefs about math. Are students more excited in math class? Do they participate more? Are they more willing to struggle on a math problem? Do I hear fewer students saying "This is so boring" or "I hate math" when I visit? I often find that changes in beliefs and attitudes precede changes in student work or test scores. You may want to give a survey to students about their feelings toward math to collect data or record comments that indicate excitement about math when you are visiting classrooms. You also may want to interview groups of students to ask how their feelings about math have changed. My favorite story about students' change in beliefs was when I was visiting a classroom and another adult in the room said, "I'm not a math person." Multiple students replied, "Everyone is a math person." This type of attitude shift has such a positive impact on students, even if it doesn't immediately show up on formal assessments.

How Is the Coaching Impacting Other Stakeholders?

Collaborative coaching impacts the teacher teams you are directly working with and their students, but it also can have a broader impact on others in the school and school community. For example, you may notice changes in the beliefs and attitudes of the administration team in the building. They may become more likely to position themselves as learners and work with the teams. They may also be more likely to suggest the use of one of the tools instead of mandating a new idea or strategy. Sometimes other teams in the school want to try these tools in their departments. For example, one English language arts team at one of my schools started their own form of lesson study after hearing from the math team about their experiences with it.

The changes may also spread to families and impact how the teams involve them. When teams are excited about the math going on in their classrooms, they may share their enthusiasm with families through newsletters or family math nights. I worked with one school whose math team focused on incorporating games into their classrooms, and they decided to invite families to come in one morning a week to be part of math game time in the classroom. Students would teach their families how to play different math games, and teachers had an opportunity to engage with families in a different way. Although this initiative wasn't something I directly worked on in our coaching, the teachers' excitement carried over to their work with families. As you reflect on your coaching work, you may want to look for the ways others in the school and community have been impacted by the shifts in the teacher teams.

IMPROVING OUR SKILLS AS COACHES

Just like teaching, coaching is a journey. I enjoy the process because I'm constantly learning from the teachers and students I work with, as well as from other coaches and administrators. As teams implement new strategies, I learn more about student thinking and about how these strategies work in different classrooms. I learn new ways the tools can be enacted by teacher teams in different contexts. I also continue to read about the research that comes out related to coaching and learn more about how other coaches are using different tools.

I also learn a lot from the missteps I make along the way. I made a lot of mistakes when I started coaching. I am so grateful to all the teachers who allowed me to make those mistakes and to the teachers who helped me learn to be better. This book grew out of my desire to share what I learned from those missteps.

When I reflect on my coaching, a very clear turning point was when I started to build upon what I knew about teaching children and tried to adapt that approach to working with teachers. From my time in the classroom, I knew that there was power in learning through discovering ideas on our own, in having opportunities to practice new strategies and skills, and in learning from one another. I built my coaching toolbox around those principles, and it made a big difference in my work. The mistakes I made led me to these tools, and when I find myself struggling with a new team or school, I often go back to these principles.

Let's take a look at our list from the Introduction again. You also may have added your own ideas to this list as you've been reading.

TEACHER LEARNING OCCURS WHEN . . .

- Teachers have opportunities to construct knowledge on their own as opposed to following a model of how to teach.
- Teachers have opportunities and time to explore different ideas and practice new skills.
- Teachers are encouraged to take risks and make mistakes.
- Teachers have opportunities to examine and discuss other teachers' work and strategies.
- Teachers sometimes work in whole groups, small groups, and individually with the coach.

STOP and JOT

 What other similarities between teacher learning and student learning have you noticed as you read through the chapters? What are some differences between the way adults and students learn?

Although a lot of similarities exist between adult learning and K–8 student learning, I hinted at a big difference in the previous chapter: *adults have to unlearn a lot more stuff*. That's not to say students don't have to unlearn a lot as well. I've had many middle-school math students who don't understand why they have to persevere through one complex problem for a whole math class instead of doing multiple mindless math drills on a worksheet. With those students, I've had to help them unlearn what it means to "do mathematics" and develop a new concept of what doing math actually entails. It's the same process with teachers, but they have been looking at the world in a certain way for much longer than students have.

I know this challenge personally because I too had to unlearn many things about math when I started teaching and to replace my old beliefs with new ideas. For example, I had to learn that faster is not better, that there are multiple ways to approach a problem, that teaching does not mean filling others' heads with the mathematical knowledge that I have but rather allowing students the joy of discovering it on their own. I had to begin to question why I always thought I was good at math in school. Did I really understand math as well as I thought I did, or was I just really good at memorizing? I see my role as a coach as helping teachers question what they believe to be true about teaching and learning. That doesn't mean that I don't value the experiences of the teachers I work with— I do! I just want to build onto those experiences. I want to allow teachers to see their students and the ways that they learn with a new lens. I want teachers to have experiences that maybe don't align with what they previously believed. I want them to have that moment where a student says, "I was sure that 15 + 25 was 30 when I used stacking, but when you give me the counters, I see it's 40. What is going on here?" I hope you've seen some of those moments in the earlier sections. The tools I've shared are the ways I try to create dissonance. I use them to engineer moments where what we always believed to be true may not be true.

I've also had to unlearn what I thought coaching was. I first thought I had to prove myself. I thought I had to be the one with all the knowledge. But just like in the classroom, I realized that it's the process of constructing knowledge together that is important. By being willing to be vulnerable and take risks myself, I allow teachers I work with to feel the same way. I've realized that being a coach is more about sitting alongside the team than it is about being in front of them. Being a coach is also about listening more than I speak.

Coaching is hard work. The dissonance we create for teachers feels terrible at times. It's easier for teams to reject ideas and push them away than it is to confront alternatives. It's easier to say that this strategy is confusing, or that it takes too much time to teach this way. It's easier to look for evidence that supports what we have been doing, because the alternative is wondering what many veteran teachers have said to me: "Have I been wrong all along? Have I been doing my students a disservice?" Most of the time, the answer is no. I like to believe that we all try to do best with what we know, but we learn new things as we go along. A surgeon looks at new research and thinks about whether the technique they are using needs to change. The same is true for us as teachers and coaches. We are constantly evolving.

Therefore, coaching is not teaching a new strategy; coaching is about providing tools to evaluate and think about new strategies together. It's about creating safe communities for teachers where they are willing to take risks and feel vulnerable. It's about curating resources and sharing new research and strategies with teachers who don't have time to read through all the new ideas that are out there. It's helping them find solutions to address needs and questions they express and then providing structures and support to learn about, implement, and reflect on those strategies. The 6 Tools in this book give you a starting point to do these things with your team. They have made the hard work of coaching more manageable for me and more rewarding. When I moved out of the classroom and into coaching, I feared that I would never be able to recreate that feeling that I had when the light bulb went off over a student's head or when students said to me, "I never liked math until this year." By using the collaborative coaching tools, however, I have enjoyed countless rewarding moments, both with teachers and with the students in their classes. I sincerely hope that the 6 Tools help you in the same way, on your own coaching journey.

APPENDICES

Design Challenge Note-Taking Template

GROUP 1	**GROUP 2**
Designer:	Designer:
Group Members:	Group Members:
Notes:	Notes:
Quotes:	Quotes:
GROUP 3	**GROUP 4**
Designer:	Designer:
Group Members:	Group Members:
Notes:	Notes:
Quotes:	Quotes:

©2023 by Nicora Placa from *6 Tools for Collaborative Mathematics Coaching*. Portsmouth, NH: Stenhouse.
Available for download at https://nicoraplaca.com/6tools/. May be reproduced for educational use.

Student Interviews Planning Template

Learning Goal for the Team:	
Step 1: Introducing student interviews to the team How will you introduce the idea of student interviews to the team? What readings or videos will you use? What discussion questions will you ask about the readings/videos?	
Step 2: Selecting task What task will you use? Why?	
Step 3: Practicing the interviews How and when will the team practice their interviewing skills? What facilitation questions will you ask after they practice interviewing one another?	
Step 4: Selecting students Which students will you interview? Why?	
Step 5: Conducting the interviews When will the interviews take place? Who will conduct them? Will you record them? What note-taking tools might you use?	
Step 6: Analyzing the interviews When will the team analyze the interviews? What guiding questions will you ask? How will you record the outcome of the analysis? What are your next steps for the team?	

©2023 by Nicora Placa from *6 Tools for Collaborative Mathematics Coaching*. Portsmouth, NH: Stenhouse. Available for download at https://nicoraplaca.com/6tools/. May be reproduced for educational use.

Visiting Classrooms Planning Template

Learning Goal for the Team:	
Step 1: Communicate with the team How will I introduce my visits to the team? Will I send an email? Will I discuss it in a team meeting? How will I frame the visits? How will I introduce myself to the students in the classroom? How will I communicate about the visits to the administration?	
Step 2: Determine a focus for visits What is the focus of my visits? What questions about student learning do I hope to answer from these visits?	
Step 3: Collect data How will I collect data? What types of data will I record? What tool will I use to take notes?	
Step 4: Analyze data How will I analyze individual classroom data? What questions will I ask as I review my notes? How will I analyze data across classrooms? What questions will I ask as I review my notes?	
Step 5: Summarize and share How will I share the findings from my visit? Who will I share them with?	

©2023 by Nicora Placa from *6 Tools for Collaborative Mathematics Coaching*. Portsmouth, NH: Stenhouse. Available for download at https://nicoraplaca.com/6tools/. May be reproduced for educational use.

Learning Walks Planning Template

Learning Goal for the Team:	
GETTING READY FOR LEARNING WALKS	
Step 1: Select who to visit and who will be visiting Where will you conduct the visits? Why? Which classrooms will be visited? Why? Who will be visiting the classrooms? Why?	
Step 2: Introduce learning walks to the team How will you introduce learning walks to the team? What readings/videos will you use to introduce them? What questions or activities will you use to debrief the readings/videos?	
Step 3: Set a focus for the visits How will you cocreate a focus for the visits? What questions or resources will guide the team in developing the focus?	
Step 4: Practice making low-inference observations What video clip will you use? What do you anticipate the team will notice? What questions will you ask to guide the team to make low-inference observations?	(continued)

©2023 by Nicora Placa from *6 Tools for Collaborative Mathematics Coaching*. Portsmouth, NH: Stenhouse.
Available for download at https://nicoraplaca.com/6tools/. May be reproduced for educational use.

Learning Walks Planning Template (continued)

THE DAY OF THE LEARNING WALK	
Step 1: Engage with the Math Before Heading Out How will you review the math tasks with the team before the visit? What student responses do you hope they anticipate? What questions will you ask as they solve the task?	
Step 2: Visit the Classrooms What schedule will you follow? What protocol will you use for the visits? How will you take notes?	
Step 3: Debrief the Learning Walk After the Classroom Visits How will you help the team individually organize the data? What guiding questions will you ask as the team analyzes the data? What prompts will you use to help the team reflect on the walk and their next steps? What did you learn from the walk about your team? What next steps do you have for the team? For individual teachers?	

©2023 by Nicora Placa from *6 Tools for Collaborative Mathematics Coaching*. Portsmouth, NH: Stenhouse. Available for download at https://nicoraplaca.com/6tools/. May be reproduced for educational use.

Rehearsing Routines Planning Template

Learning Goal for the Team:	
GETTING READY FOR LEARNING WALKS	
Step 1: Choose a routine Which routine and why?	
Step 2: Learn about the routine How will we learn about routines? (books, articles, video sources) What facilitation questions will I ask as we learn about the routines?	
Step 3: Plan and rehearse the routine How will we plan the routine together? How will I rehearse the routines? How will I strategically group the team members as they rehearse? What facilitation questions will I ask as we rehearse the routine?	
Step 4: Implement the routine with students How will we try the routine out with students? In small groups? Whole class? Will we videotape or watch live? What note-takers will I have the team use as they watch the routines?	
Step 5: Reflect and plan next steps How will we debrief our experiences of trying out the routines with students? What questions will facilitate the learning? How will I assess learning and plan next steps for the team? Who would benefit from one-on-one coaching or planning support? How can I pair certain people up to learn from one another?	

©2023 by Nicora Placa from *6 Tools for Collaborative Mathematics Coaching*. Portsmouth, NH: Stenhouse. Available for download at https://nicoraplaca.com/6tools/. May be reproduced for educational use.

Lesson Study Planning Template

Team members:	
Introducing lesson study How will I introduce the idea of lesson study to the team? What readings or videos will help support this introduction?	
Step 1: Develop a research question What are our goals for our students? What do we want to focus our research on to meet these goals? What research question do we want to center our lesson study around?	
Step 2: Research our question What books, articles, or materials should I have available? What learning do I need to do? What facilitation questions will I ask as we investigate the resources?	
Step 3: Plan and rehearse How will we plan the lesson? When? What templates can I share that will help focus the planning? Will we rehearse the plan? How? When?	
Step 4: Implement How will I schedule the implementation of the lesson? Who will teach it? What will the observers do? What will be my role during the implementation? How will we capture our learning? What note-takers will be available for the team to use as they watch the lesson?	
Step 5: Debrief How will we debrief our experiences? Will we use a protocol? What questions will I ask that will facilitate the learning?	
Step 6: Share and summarize How will we summarize and share our findings?	

©2023 by Nicora Placa from *6 Tools for Collaborative Mathematics Coaching*. Portsmouth, NH: Stenhouse.
Available for download at https://nicoraplaca.com/6tools/. May be reproduced for educational use.

Lesson Study Lesson Planning Template

PART ONE: GENERAL INFORMATION

Team Members Lesson facilitator: Other participants:	Research question:
Topic:	**Implementation date:**

Standards addressed: (Please give brief descriptions as well as standard numbers and grade level.)

What are the goals for this lesson? (Note: Lesson goals should reflect the department's research goal.)

Assessment items: How will you assess student understanding during and at the end of the lesson?

What prior knowledge do students bring to this task?

What language supports and special education modifications are relevant to this lesson?

©2023 by Nicora Placa from *6 Tools for Collaborative Mathematics Coaching*. Portsmouth, NH: Stenhouse.
Available for download at https://nicoraplaca.com/6tools/. May be reproduced for educational use.

Lesson Study Lesson Planning Template (continued)

PART TWO: LESSON OUTLINE			
Lesson Part I: Launch			
Prompts, questions (What will the teacher say and do?)	Anticipated responses (What might students say and do?)	How will the teacher react to students' responses?	Goal for this element/ time allocation/ miscellaneous

Lesson Part II: Explore			
Prompts, questions (What will the teacher say and do?)	Anticipated responses (What might students say and do?)	How will the teacher react to students' responses?	Goal for this element/ time allocation/ miscellaneous

Lesson Part III: Share/Summarize			
Prompts, questions (What will the teacher say and do?)	Anticipated responses (What might students say and do?)	How will the teacher react to students' responses?	Goal for this element/ time allocation/ miscellaneous

©2023 by Nicora Placa from *6 Tools for Collaborative Mathematics Coaching*. Portsmouth, NH: Stenhouse.
Available for download at https://nicoraplaca.com/6tools/. May be reproduced for educational use.

Lesson Study Note-Taking Template

Research question:
Success criteria/look-fors: What are our "look-fors" in terms of our research goal?
What is my role in observing? What am I focusing on (i.e., certain group of students, student-to-student talk, participation)?

NOTES SECTION		
Time	Notice	Wonder

©2023 by Nicora Placa from *6 Tools for Collaborative Mathematics Coaching*. Portsmouth, NH: Stenhouse.
Available for download at https://nicoraplaca.com/6tools/. May be reproduced for educational use.

REFERENCES

Aguilar, Elena. 2016. *The Art Of Coaching Teams: Building Resilient Communities That Transform Schools.* San Francisco, CA: Jossey-Bass, A Wiley Brand.

Ball, Deborah Loewenberg, and Hyman Bass. 2022. "Toward a Practice-Based Theory of Mathematical Knowledge for Teaching." In *Proceedings of the 2002 annual meeting of the Canadian Mathematics Education Study Group,* pp. 3–14.

Ball, Deborah Loewenberg, Sarah T. Lubienski, and Denise S. Mewborn. 2001. "Research on Teaching Mathematics: The Unsolved Problem of Teachers' Mathematical Knowledge." *Handbook of Research on Teaching* 4: 433–456.

Barnhart, Tara, and Elizabeth van Es. 2015. "Studying Teacher Noticing: Examining the Relationship Among Pre-Service Science Teachers' Ability to Attend, Analyze, and Respond to Student Thinking." *Teaching and Teacher Education* 45: 83–93.

Borko, Hilda. 2004. "Professional Development and Teacher Learning: Mapping the Terrain." *Educational Researcher* 33 (8): 3–15.

Brodie, Karin. 2013. "The Power of Professional Learning Communities." *Education as Change* 17 (1): 5–18.

Burns, Marilyn, and Lynn Zolli. 2021. *Listening to Learn.* Portsmouth, NH: Heinemann.

Buschman, Larry. 2001. "Research, Reflection, Practice: December 2001: Using Student Interviews to Guide Classroom Instruction: An Action Research Project." *Teaching Children Mathematics* 8 (4): 222–227.

Bushart, Brian. "Numberless Word Problems." https://bstockus.wordpress.com/numberless-word-problems/.

Cameron, Antonia. 2020. *Early Childhood Math Routines: Empowering Young Minds to Think*. Portland, ME: Stenhouse.

Carpenter, Thomas P., Elizabeth Fennema, Megan Loef Franke, Linda Levi, and Susan B. Empson. 2014. *Children's Mathematics: Cognitively Guided Instruction*. Portsmouth, NH: Heinemann.

Cervone, Laureen, and Patricia Martinez-Miller. 2007. "Classroom Walk-throughs as a Catalyst for School Improvement." *Leadership Compass* 4 (4): 1–4.

City, Elizabeth A., Richard F. Elmore, Sarah E. Fiarman, and Lee Teitel. 2009. *Instructional Rounds in Education: A Network Approach to Improving Teaching and Learning*. Vol. 30. Cambridge, MA: Harvard Education Press.

Cohen, Elisabeth G., and Rachel A. Lotan. 2014. *Designing Groupwork: Strategies for the Heterogeneous Classroom*. 3rd. ed. New York: Teachers College Press.

Danielson, Christopher. 2018. *How Many?: A Counting Book*. Portland, ME: Stenhouse.

———. 2016 *Which One Doesn't Belong?: Playing with Shapes*. Portland, ME: Stenhouse.

Danks, Shelby, Jennifer Wilson, Max Ray-Riek, Kristin Gray, and Kevin Liner. 2021. The Illustrative Mathematics Implementation Reflection Tool (for Grades K–5). Oro Valley, AZ: Illustrative Mathematics.

Darling-Hammond, Linda, Dion Burns, Carol Campbell, A. Lin Goodwin, Karen Hammerness, Ee-Ling Low, Ann McIntyre, Mistilina Sato, and Ken Zeichner. 2017. *Empowered Educators: How High-Performing Systems Shape Teaching Quality Around the World*. San Francisco, CA: John Wiley & Sons.

Del Prete, Thomas. 2013. *Teacher Rounds: A Guide to Collaborative Learning in and from Practice*. Thousand Oaks, CA: Corwin Press.

Desimone, Laura M. 2009. "Improving Impact Studies of Teachers' Professional Development: Toward Better Conceptualizations and Measures." *Educational Researcher* 38 (3): 181–199.

Desimone, Laura M., and Katie Pak. 2017. "Instructional Coaching as High-Quality Professional Development." *Theory into Practice* 56 (1): 3–12.

Drake, Corey, Tonia J. Land, Tonya Gau Bartell, Julia M. Aguirre, Mary Q. Foote, Amy Roth McDuffie, and Erin E. Turner. 2015. "Three Strategies for Opening Curriculum Spaces." *Teaching Children Mathematics* 21 (6): 346–353.

Erickson, Frederick. 2011. "On Noticing Teacher Noticing." In *Mathematics Teacher Noticing*, 47–64. London: Routledge.

Erickson, Tim. 1989. *Get it Together: Math Problems for Groups, Grades 4–12.* Berkeley, CA: EQUALS.

Erickson, Tim. 1995. *United We Solve: 116 Math Problems for Groups, Grades 5–10.* Oakland, CA: eeps media.

Fisher, Douglas, and Nancy Frey. 2014. "Using Teacher Learning Walks to Improve Instruction." *Principal Leadership* 14 (5): 58–61.

Franke, Megan Loef, and Elham Kazemi. 2001. "Teaching as Learning Within a Community of Practice: Characterizing Generative Growth." *Beyond Classical Pedagogy in Elementary Mathematics: The Nature of Facilitative Teaching*, 61–88. London: Routledge.

Franke, Meghan L., Elham Kazemi, and Angela Chan Turrou. 2018. *Choral Counting and Counting Collections: Transforming the PreK–5 Math Classroom.* Portland, ME: Stenhouse.

Gallucci, Chrysan, Michelle DeVoogt Van Lare, Irene H. Yoon, and Beth Boatright. 2010. "Instructional Coaching: Building Theory About the Role and Organizational Support for Professional Learning." *American Educational Research Journal* 47 (4): 919–963.

Gamoran Sherin, Miriam, and Elizabeth A. van Es. 2009. "Effects of Video Club Participation on Teachers' Professional Vision." *Journal of Teacher Education* 60 (1): 20–37.

Gawande, Atul. 2011. "Personal Best." *The New Yorker* 3: 44–53.

Ghousseini, Hala. 2017. "Rehearsals of Teaching and Opportunities to Learn Mathematical Knowledge for Teaching." *Cognition and Instruction* 35 (3): 188–211.

Ghousseini, Hala, Sarah Schneider Kavanagh, Elizabeth Dutro, and Elham Kazemi. 2022. "The Fourth Wall of Professional Learning and Cultures of Collaboration." *Educational Researcher* 51 (3): 216–222.

Gibbons, Lynsey K., and Paul Cobb. 2017. "Focusing on Teacher Learning Opportunities to Identify Potentially Productive Coaching Activities." *Journal of Teacher Education* 68 (4): 411–425.

Gibbons, Lynsey K., Elham Kazemi, and Rebecca M. Lewis. 2017. "Developing Collective Capacity to Improve Mathematics Instruction: Coaching as a Lever for School-Wide Improvement." *The Journal of Mathematical Behavior* 46: 231–250.

Ginsberg, Margery B., and Damon Murphy. 2002. "How Walkthroughs Open Doors." *Educational Leadership* 59 (8): 34–36.

Ginsberg, Margery, Olimpia Bahena, Jessica Kertz, and Iysha Jones. 2018. "Motivation in Motion." *The Learning Professional* 39 (3): 38–46.

Ginsburg, Herbert. 1997. *Entering the Child's Mind: The Clinical Interview in Psychological Research and Practice.* Cambridge, UK: Cambridge University Press.

Grossman, Pamela, Samuel Wineburg, and Stephen Woolworth. 2001. "Toward a Theory of Teacher Community." *Teachers College Record* 103 (6): 942–1012.

Heng, Mary Anne, and Akhila Sudarshan. 2013. "'Bigger Number Means You Plus!'—Teachers Learning to Use Clinical Interviews to Understand Students' Mathematical Thinking." *Educational Studies in Mathematics* 83 (3): 471–485.

Humphreys, Cathy, and Ruth Parker. 2015. *Making Number Talks Matter: Developing Mathematical Practices and Deepening Understanding, Grades 4–10.* Portland, ME: Stenhouse.

Hunting, Robert P. 1997. "Clinical Interview Methods in Mathematics Education Research and Practice." *The Journal of Mathematical Behavior* 16 (2): 145–165.

Jacobs, Victoria R., Megan Loef Franke, Thomas P. Carpenter, Linda Levi, and Dan Battey. 2007. "Professional Development Focused on Children's Algebraic Reasoning in Elementary School." *Journal for Research in Mathematics Education* 38 (3): 258–288.

Jacobs, Victoria R., and Susan B. Empson. 2016. "Responding to Children's Mathematical Thinking in the Moment: An Emerging Framework of Teaching Moves." *ZDM* 48 (1): 185–197.

Kachur, Donald S., Judith A. Stout, and Claudia L. Edwards. 2010. *Classroom Walkthroughs to Improve Teaching and Learning.* Larchmont, NY: Eye on Education.

———. 2013. *Engaging Teachers in Classroom Walkthroughs.* Alexandria, VA: ASCD.

Kang, Hosun, and Charles W. Anderson. 2015. "Supporting Preservice Science Teachers' Ability to Attend and Respond to Student Thinking by Design." *Science Education* 99 (5): 863–895.

Kanold, Timothy D., Mona Toncheff, Matthew R. Larson, Bill Barnes, Jessica Kanold-McIntyre, and Sarah Schuhl. 2018. "Mathematics Coaching and Collaboration in a PLC at Work. Every Student Can Learn Mathematics." Bloomington, IN: Solution Tree

Kavanagh, Sarah Schneider, Chauncey Monte-Sano, Abby Reisman, Brad Fogo, Sarah McGrew, and Peter Cipparone. 2019. "Teaching Content in Practice: Investigating Rehearsals of Social Studies Discussions." *Teaching and Teacher Education* 86: 1–11.

Kazemi, Elham, Hala Ghousseini, Adrian Cunard, and Angela Chan Turrou. 2016. "Getting Inside Rehearsals: Insights from Teacher Educators to Support Work on Complex Practice." *Journal of Teacher Education* 67 (1): 18–31.

Kazemi, Elham, L. K. Gibbons, Rebecca Lewis, Alison Fox, A. B. Hintz, Megan Kelley-Petersen, and R. Balf. 2018. "Math Labs: Teachers, Teacher Educators, and School Leaders Learning Together with and from Their Own Students." *Journal of Mathematics Education Leadership* 19 (1): 23–36.

Kazemi, Elham, Lynsey K. Gibbons, Kendra Lomax, and Megan L. Franke. 2016. "Listening to and Learning from Student Thinking." *Teaching Children Mathematics* 23 (3): 182–190.

Kazemi, Elham, and Amanda Hubbard. 2008. "New Directions for the Design and Study of Professional Development: Attending to the Coevolution of Teachers' Participation Across Contexts." *Journal of Teacher Education* 59 (5): 428–441.

Kazemi, Elham, and Kjersti Wæge. 2015. "Learning to Teach Within Practice-Based Methods Courses." *Mathematics Teacher Education and Development* 17 (2): 125–145.

Kelemanik, Grace, Amy Lucenta, and Susan Janssen Creighton. 2016. *Routines for Reasoning: Fostering the Mathematical Practices in All Students.* Portsmouth, NH: Heinemann.

King, M. Bruce, and Fred M. Newmann. 2001. "Building School Capacity Through Professional Development: Conceptual and Empirical Considerations." *International Journal of Educational Management* 15 (2): 86–94.

Knight, Jim. 2009. "Coaching." *The Learning Professional* 30 (1): 18.

Lampert, Magdalene, Megan Loef Franke, Elham Kazemi, Hala Ghousseini, Angela Chan Turrou, Heather Beasley, Adrian Cunard, and Kathleen Crowe. 2013. "Keeping It Complex: Using Rehearsals to Support Novice Teacher Learning of Ambitious Teaching." *Journal of Teacher Education* 64 (3): 226–243.

Lemons, Richard W., and Deborah Helsing. 2009. "Learning to Walk, Walking To Learn: Reconsidering the Walkthrough as an Improvement Strategy." *Phi Delta Kappan* 90 (7): 478–484.

Lewis, C., and J. Hurd. 2011. *Lesson Study Step by Step: How Teacher Learning Communities Improve Instruction.* Portsmouth, NH: Heinemann.

Lewis, Catherine. 2002. "Does Lesson Study Have a Future in the United States?" *Nagoya Journal of Education and Human Development* 1 (1): 1–23.

Lewis, Catherine, and Rebecca Perry. 2014. "Lesson Study with Mathematical Resources: A Sustainable Model for Locally-Led Teacher Professional Learning." *Mathematics Teacher Education and Development* 16 (1): n1.

Lewis, Catherine C., and Ineko Tsuchida. 1998. "A Lesson Is Like a Swiftly Flowing River: How Research Lessons Improve Japanese Education." *American Educator* 22 (4): 12–17; 50–52.

Lynsey, K. Gibbons, Elham Kazemi, and Rebecca M. Lewis. 2017. "Developing Collective Capacity to Improve Mathematics Instruction: Coaching as a Lever for School-Wide Improvement." *The Journal of Mathematical Behavior* 46: 231–250.

Mangin, Melinda M., and KaiLonnie Dunsmore. 2015. "How the Framing of Instructional Coaching as a Lever for Systemic or Individual Reform Influences the Enactment of Coaching." *Educational Administration Quarterly* 51 (2): 179–213.

Mason, John. 2002. *Researching Your Own Practice: The Discipline of Noticing.* London: Routledge.

McCoy, Ann C., Joann Barnett, and Emily X. Combs. 2013. *High-Yield Routines for Grades K–8.* Reston, VA: National Council of Teachers of Mathematics.

McDonald, Morva, Elham Kazemi, and Sarah Schneider Kavanagh. 2013. "Core Practices and Pedagogies of Teacher Education: A Call for a Common Language and Collective Activity." *Journal of Teacher Education* 64 (5): 378–386.

McDonough, Andrea, Barbara Clarke, and Doug M. Clarke. 2002. "Understanding, Assessing, and Developing Children's Mathematical Thinking: The Power of a One-To-One Interview for Preservice Teachers in Providing Insights into Appropriate Pedagogical Practices." *International Journal of Educational Research* 37 (2): 211–226.

McGatha, Maggie B., Ryan Davis, and Amy Stokes-Levine. 2015. "The Impact of Mathematics Coaching on Teachers and Students." National Council of Teachers of Mathematics Research Briefs.

Moss, Connie M., and Susan M. Brookhart. 2013. "A New View of Walk-Throughs." *Educational Leadership* 70 (7): 42–45.

National Council of Teachers of Mathematics (NTSM). 2000. Principles and Standards for School Mathematics. Reston, VA: National Council of Teachers of Mathematics.

Parker, Ruth E., and Cathy Humphreys. 2018. *Digging Deeper: Making Number Talks Matter Even More, Grades 3–10.* Portland, ME: Stenhouse.

Parrish, Sherry. 2022a. *Number Talks: Whole Number Computation.* Portsmouth, NH: Heinemann.

Parrish, Sherry. 2022b. *Number Talks: Fractions, Decimals and Percentages*. Portsmouth, NH: Heinemann.

Perry, Rebecca R., and Catherine C. Lewis. 2009. "What Is Successful Adaptation of Lesson Study in the U.S.?" *Journal of Educational Change* 10 (4): 365–391.

Placa, Nicora. 2020. "Learn to Listen." *The Learning Professional* 41 (1): 32–35.

Ray-Riek, Max. 2013. *Powerful Problem Solving: Activities for Sense Making with the Mathematical Practices*. Portsmouth, NH: Heinemann.

Rinke, Carol R., and Divonna M. Stebick. 2013. "'Not Just Learning About It But Actually Doing It': The Evolution of a Teacher Inquiry Culture." *Action in Teacher Education* 35 (1): 72–84.

Ronfeldt, Matthew, Susanna Owens Farmer, Kiel McQueen, and Jason A. Grissom. 2015. "Teacher Collaboration in Instructional Teams and Student Achievement." *American Educational Research Journal* 52 (3): 475–514.

Santagata, Rossella, and Cathery Yeh. 2016. "The Role of Perception, Interpretation, and Decision Making in the Development of Beginning Teachers' Competence." *ZDM* 48 (1): 153–165.

Schoenfeld, A. H., and the Teaching for Robust Understanding Project. 2016. "An Introduction to the Teaching for Robust Understanding (TRU) Framework." Berkeley, CA: Graduate School of Education. Retrieved from http://truframework.org or http://map.mathshell.org/trumath.php.

Schoenfeld, Alan H. 2011. "Noticing Matters. A Lot. Now What?" In *Mathematics Teacher Noticing*, 253–268. London: Routledge.

Selkrig, Mark, and Kim Keamy. 2015. "Promoting a Willingness to Wonder: Moving from Congenial to Collegial Conversations That Encourage Deep and Critical Reflection for Teacher Educators." *Teachers and Teaching* 21 (4): 421–436.

Sherin, Miriam Gamoran, and Victoria R. Jacobs. 2011. "Situating the Study of Teacher Noticing." In *Mathematics Teacher Noticing*, 33–44. London: Routledge.

Sherin, Miriam, and Elizabeth van Es. 2005. "Using Video to Support Teachers' Ability to Notice Classroom Interactions." *Journal of Technology and Teacher Education* 13 (3): 475–491.

Shumway, Jessica F. 2018. *Number Sense Routines: Building Mathematical Understanding Every Day in Grades 3–5.* Portland, ME: Stenhouse.

———. 2011. *Number Sense Routines: Building Numerical Literacy Every Day in Grades K–3.* Portland, ME: Stenhouse.

Stahnke, Rebekka, Sven Schueler, and Bettina Roesken-Winter. 2016. "Teachers' Perception, Interpretation, And Decision-Making: A Systematic Review Of Empirical Mathematics Education Research." *ZDM* 48 (1): 1–27.

Stepanek, Jennifer Smith, Gary Appel, Melinda Leong, Michelle Turner Mangan, and Mark Mitchell. 2006. *Leading Lesson Study: A Practical Guide for Teachers and Facilitators.* Thousand Oaks, CA: Corwin.

Stephens, Max. 2011. "Ensuring Instruction Changes: Evidence Based Teaching–How Can Lesson Study Inform Coaching, Instructional Rounds, and Learning Walks." *Journal of Science and Mathematics Education in Southeast Asia* 34 (1): 111–133.

Stigler, James W., and James Hiebert. 2009. *The Teaching Gap: Best Ideas from the World's Teachers for Improving Education in the Classroom.* New York: Free Press.

Sweeney, Diane, and Leanna S. Harris. 2020. *The Essential Guide for Student-Centered Coaching: What Every K–12 Coach and School Leader Needs to Know.* Thousand Oaks, CA: Corwin.

Takahashi, Akihiko. 2000. "Current Trends and Issues in Lesson Study in Japan and the United States." *Journal of Japan Society of Mathematical Education* 82 (12): 15–21.

Takahashi, Akihiko, and Thomas McDougal. 2016. "Collaborative Lesson Research: Maximizing the Impact of Lesson Study." *ZDM* 48 (4): 513–526.

Takahashi, Akihiko, and Makoto Yoshida. 2004. "Ideas for Establishing Lesson-Study Communities." *Teaching Children Mathematics* 10 (9): 436–443.

Tobias, Sheila. 1993. *Overcoming Math Anxiety.* New York: WW Norton & Company.

van Es, Elizabeth A., and Miriam G. Sherin. 2021. "Expanding on Prior Conceptualizations of Teacher Noticing." *ZDM–Mathematics Education* 53 (1): 17–27.

van Es, Elizabeth A., and Miriam Gamoran Sherin. 2010. "The Influence of Video Clubs on Teachers' Thinking and Practice." *Journal of Mathematics Teacher Education* 13 (2): 155–176.

Vescio, Vicki, Dorene Ross, and Alyson Adams. 2008. "A Review of Research on the Impact of Professional Learning Communities on Teaching Practice and Student Learning." *Teaching and Teacher Education* 24 (1): 80–91.

Wæge, Kjersti, and Janne Fauskanger. 2021. "Teacher Time Outs in Rehearsals: In-Service Teachers Learning Ambitious Mathematics Teaching Practices." *Journal of Mathematics Teacher Education* 24 (6): 563–586.

Webb, Jared, and P. Holt Wilson. 2022. "Designing Rehearsals for Secondary Mathematics Teachers to Refine Practice." *Mathematics Teacher Educator* 10 (2): 129–142.

West, Lucy, and Antonia Cameron. 2013. *Agents of Change: How Content Coaching Transforms Teaching and Learning.* Portsmouth, NH: Heinemann.

Wujec, Tom. 2010 "Build a Tower. Build a Team." https://www.ted.com/talks/tom_wujec_build_a_tower_build_a_team?language=en

Yoshida, Makoto. 1999. "Lesson Study: An Ethnographic Investigation of School-based Teacher Development in Japan." Unpublished doctoral dissertation, University of Chicago.

INDEX